澳新加诗佳韵

连巧红　黄建滨　编译

ZHEJIANG UNIVERSITY PRESS
浙江大学出版社
·杭州·

图书在版编目(CIP)数据

澳新加诗佳韵 / 连巧红，黄建滨编译. -- 杭州：
浙江大学出版社，2024. 6. -- ISBN 978-7-308-25115-0

Ⅰ. H319.4

中国国家版本馆 CIP 数据核字第 2024BD6651 号

澳新加诗佳韵

连巧红　黄建滨　编译

责任编辑	诸葛勤
责任校对	郑成业
封面设计	周　灵
出版发行	浙江大学出版社
	（杭州市天目山路 148 号　邮政编码 310007）
	（网址：http://www.zjupress.com）
排　　版	浙江大千时代文化传媒有限公司
印　　刷	浙江新华数码印务有限公司
开　　本	787 mm×1092 mm　1/32
印　　张	9
字　　数	224 千
版 印 次	2024 年 6 月第 1 版　2024 年 6 月第 1 次印刷
书　　号	ISBN　978-7-308-25115-0
定　　价	78.00 元

Contents / 目　录

澳大利亚诗歌选译

Lachesis
算命者

Mary Gilmore（1865—1962）

Eve Song
夏娃

Never Admit the Pain
绝不承认痛苦

An Aboriginal Simile
一个关于土著的比喻

Old Botany Bay
老博塔尼湾

An Allegory
寓言故事

Nationality
我们是同宗

The Tenancy
房主承租

新西兰诗歌选译

Darcy Cresswell（1896—1960）

O England

英格兰

Summer's Sadness

夏日悲歌

Arthur Rex Duggard Fairburn（1904—1957）

Winter Night

冷冬夜

Tapu

禁忌

A Farewell

再不见

The Encounter

偶然相遇

I'm Older than You, Please Listen

请你聆听，老者之言

罗宾·海德诗一首······················170

The Deserted Village
荒废了的村庄

Charles Brasch（1909—1973）
查尔斯·布拉什诗五首······················174

The Islands
这些岛

Envoy's Report
特使公告

Forerunners
先行者

The Silent Land
沉默土地

Great Sea
大海

加拿大诗歌选译

The Rapid
湍流颂

Brock
奠

The Twofold Victory
双重的大胜仗

The Light in the Window Pane
窗玻璃透出的光

The Little Shoes
一双小鞋

Despondency
意志消沉

The Red-Men—A Sonnet
红种人——十四行（诗）

Afoot
徒步

In an Old Barn
在旧谷仓

The Aim
目标

The Potato Harvest
马铃薯大丰收

The Great and Little Weavers
伟大渺小的织工

Disarmament
放下武器

Red Moon
红月

A Poem to Pony
致波妮的诗句

澳大利亚诗歌选译

Anonymous
无名氏诗三首

Moreton Bay

One Sunday morning as I went walking, by Brisbane waters I
   chanced to stray;

I heard a prisoner his fate bewailing, as on the sunny river bank
   he lay:

"I am a native of Erin's island and banished now from my native
   shore;

They tore me from my aged parents and from the maiden whom
   I do adore.

"I've been a prisoner at Port Macquarie, at Norfolk Island and
   Emu Plains,

At Castle Hill and at cursed Toongabbie, at all those settlements
   I've worked in chains;

But of all places of condemnation and penal stations of New
South Wales,

To Moreton Bay I have found no equal; excessive tyranny each
day prevails.

"For three long years I was beastly treated, and heavy irons on
my legs I wore;

My back with flogging is lacerated and often painted with my
crimson gore.

And many a man from downright starvation lies mouldering now
underneath the clay;

And Captain Logan he had us mangled at the triangles of
Moreton Bay.

"Like the Egyptians and ancient Hebrews we were oppressed
under Logan's yoke,

Till a native black lying there in ambush did give our tyrant his
mortal stroke,

My fellow prisoners, be exhilarated that all such monsters such a
death may find!

And when from bondage we are liberated our former sufferings
shall fade from mind."

莫尔顿湾

我漫步在布里斯班水域，迷路在一个周日清晨；
恰遇见一名囚犯躺在阳光明媚的河边，在悲叹命运：
"我是艾琳岛土生土长的人，却被放逐远离故乡；
不能陪伴在年迈的父母和心爱的少女身旁。

"我曾被关在麦夸里港、诺福克岛和伊姆平原监狱，
城堡山和被诅咒的图恩加比，戴枷锁做活；
在新南威尔士这些地方饱受责难和惩戒，
但没有一处堪比莫尔顿湾监狱；那里每天暴行肆虐。

"漫长三年，我惨遭非人对待，腿上戴着沉重的铁链；
后背被他们鞭打得伤痕累累，全身是暗红色血斑。
多少人被活活地饿死现已变成泥土下的腐骨；
多少人在莫尔顿湾三角地带被洛根上尉屠戮。

"我们饱受洛根的压迫，像埃及人和古希伯来人，
直到一个黑人土著出其不意，给了暴君致命一击。
我的囚犯同胞，让我们为这些禽兽们的死亡振臂欢呼！
当我们不再被监禁后，曾经的苦难记忆也终将淡去。"

The Streets of Forbes

Come all you Lachlan men, and a sorrowful tale I'll tell
Concerning of a hero bold who through misfortune fell.
His name it was Ben Hall, a man of good renown
Who was hunted from his station, and like a dog shot down.

Three years he roamed the roads, and he showed the traps some
    fun;
A thousand pound was on his head, with Gilbert and Jon Dunn.
Ben parted from his comrades, the outlaws did agree
To give away bushranging and to cross the briny sea.

Ben went to Goobang Creek, and that was his downfall;
For riddled like a sieve was valiant Ben Hall.
'T was early in the morning upon the fifth of May
When the seven police surrounded him as fast asleep as he lay.

Bill Dargin he was chosen to shoot the outlaw dead;
The troopers then fired madly, and filled him full of lead.
They rolled him in a blanket, and strapped him to his prad,
And led him through the streets of Forbes to show the prize they
    had.

福布斯街

来吧拉克伦人，我讲个悲伤的传闻
有关一个不幸而倒下的孤胆英雄。
他的名字叫本·霍尔，有点名气
因追捕而逃亡，却像狗一样被击毙。

三年来他在街上游荡，笑对罗网；
与吉尔伯特、乔·邓恩，被悬赏千镑。
本和他的同伴们分开，他们打算
放弃丛林探险，逃去咸海的另一边。

本去了古邦溪，那是他的失误；
英勇的霍尔子弹全身遍布。
那个时候是五月五日的凌晨
当七名警察将他团团包围他正酣睡梦中。

比尔·达金先开枪射杀这名好汉；
警察们疯狂射击，把他灌满铅弹。
他们把他裹在毯子里，绑上马背，
穿过福布斯街，将战果向人们展现。

Much Distressed

"Her Majesty the Queen was much distressed at the terrible news of the wreck of the steamer Elbe."

The noisy urchins scampered round
　　Amidst the careless crowd:
"An awful wreck! Three hundred drown'd!"
　　They cried the news aloud.
We bought a paper, paused, and read
　　With melancholy zest,
Then winked our other eye, and said—
　　"The Queen will be distressed."

We felt it coming from the first;
　　Court flunkeys took the hint,
And promptly got a royal burst
　　Of sorrow into print.
The cable told the touching tale
　　Exactly as we guessed—
We never knew her grief to fail,
　　The Queen was much distressed.

In time of war, should British blood

　　Be shed by niggers mean;
Or when an earthquake, or a flood
　　Appears upon the scene;
Or accidents in mines excite
　　Some public interest;
Then, posing in a blaze of light,
　　The Queen is much distressed.

很悲伤

　　"女王陛下在获知'易北号'轮船的不幸沉没后表示很悲伤。"

报童们在淡漠人群
　　之中四处叫喊:
"沉船了! 遇难三百人!"
　　卖报, 他们高喊。
我们买报, 停下双脚
　　满怀悲切翻阅,
眨了眨一只眼睛, 道——
　　"女王定会很伤悲。"

我们感觉她会哀痛;
　　王室仆人领会,
即刻将皇室的汹涌

悲痛付诸报纸。
电讯讲述感伤故事
　恰如我们所想——
我们不知她的伤悲，
　女王非常悲伤。

战时，英国人因卑微
　黑人正在流血；
或当有地震，或洪水
　在袭来的时刻；
或矿难的消息引起
　公众轰动之时；
闪光灯中，摆出姿势，
　女王非常伤悲。

Adam Lindsay Gordon（1833—1870）
亚当·林赛·戈登诗一首

The Song of the Surf

White steeds of ocean, that leap with a hollow and wearisome roar

On the bar of ironstone steep, not a fathom's length from the shore,

Is there never a seer nor sophist can interpret your wild refrain,

When speech the harshest and roughest is seldom studied in vain?

My ears are constantly smitten by that dreary monotone, in a hieroglyphic 'tis written—'tis spoken in a tongue unknown;

Gathering, growing, and swelling, and surging, and shivering, say!

What is the tale you are telling? What is the drift of your lay?

You come, and your crests are hoary with the foam of your

countless years,

You break, with a rainbow of glory, through the spray of your
glittering tears.

Is your song a song of gladness? A paean of joyous might?

Or a wail of discordant sadness for the wrongs you never can right?

For the empty seat by the ingle? For children 'reft of their sire?

For the bride sitting sad, and single, and pale, by the flickering fire?

For your ravenous pools of suction? For your shattering billow swell?

For your ceaseless work of destruction? For your hunger insatiable?

Not far from this very place, on the sand and the shingle dry,

He lay, with his batter'd face upturned to the frowning sky.

When your waters wash'd and swill'd high over his drowning
head,

When his nostrils and lungs were filled, when his feet and hands
were as lead,

When against the rock he was hurl'd, and suck'd again to the sea,

On the shores of another world, on the brink of eternity,

On the verge of annihilation, did it come to that swimmer strong,

The sudden interpretation of your mystical, weird-like song?

"Mortal! That which thou askest, ask not thou of the waves;

Fool! Thou foolishly taskest us—we are only slaves;

Might, more mighty, impels us—we must our lot fulfil,

He who gathers and swells us curbs us, too, at His will.

Think'st thou the wave that shatters questioneth His decree?

Little to us it matters, and naught it matters to thee.

Not thus, murmuring idly, we from our duty would swerve,

Over the world spread widely ever we labour and serve."

海浪的歌声

大海中的白色骏马们，发出沉闷的咆哮

在坚硬峭壁上跳跃，离海岸不足一英寻，

竟从未有预言家或智者解读你狂野话语，

而研究最凶猛粗鲁的言语鲜有徒劳？

我的双耳总是因那单调乏味的声音困扰，

象形文字写着——它说的是一种未知的语言；

凝聚着，生长着，膨胀着，涌动着，颤抖着，说！

你在讲着什么故事？你叙述的是什么？

你来了，岁月悠久的泡沫令你羽冠白皙

你破碎了，化成晶莹的泪珠，带来绚美的彩虹。

你唱的是欢乐颂歌？欢乐力量的赞歌？

还是对你那永远无法纠正的错误的悲叹？

火炉旁消失的身影？子对父的怀念？

坐在摇曳炉火旁悲伤、孤独、苍白的新娘？

为你滔滔的水流？为你惊天动地的巨浪？

为你无尽的毁灭力？永不满足的吞噬？

离此处不远的地方，干燥的沙滩上，
他平躺着，一脸沧桑看着褶皱的天空。
当你的潮水深深没过他的头顶时，
浸满鼻孔和肺部，当手脚像铅一样重，
当你将他猛甩在岩石上，又冲进海里，
在另一个世界的海岸，在那永恒的边缘，
在一切似都被摧毁之际，那个游泳健将，
是否豁然领悟你神秘、怪异的歌曲？

"人子啊！你所求的，莫要问海浪；
蠢人！不要苛求——我们仅是奴仆；
力量，更有力，驱使我们——历经磨难，
他凝聚又膨胀，任意地，设下限制。
浪花飞溅是为了质疑他的法令？
对我们来说无关紧要，对你亦然。
我们漫不经心呢喃，并非因此，逃避职责，
我们在广阔世界里恪尽职守劳作。"

Henry Kendall（1839—1882）
亨利·肯德尔诗四首

The Last of His Tribe

He crouches, and buries his face on his knees,
　　And hides in the dark of his hair;
For he cannot look up to the storm-smitten trees,
　　Or think of the loneliness there—
　　Of the loss and the loneliness there.

The wallaroos grope through the tufts of the grass,
　　And turn to their covers for fear;
But he sits in the ashes and lets them pass
　　Where the boomerangs sleep with the spear—
　　With the nullah, the sling, and the spear.

Uloola, behold him! The thunder that breaks
　　On the tops of the rocks with the rain,

And the wind which drives up with the salt of the lakes,

Have made him a hunter again—

A hunter and fisher again.

For his eyes have been full with a smouldering thought;

But he dreams of the hunts of yore,

And of foes that he sought, and of fights that he fought

With those who will battle no more—

Who will go to the battle no more.

It is well that the water which tumbles and fills

Goes moaning and moaning along;

For an echo rolls out from the sides of the hills,

And he starts at a wonderful song—

At the sounds of a wonderful song.

And he sees, through the rents of the scattering fogs,

The corroboree warlike and grim,

And the lubra who sat by the fire on the logs,

To watch, like mourner, for him:

Like a mother and mourner, for him.

Will he go in his sleep from these desolate lands,

Like a chief, to the rest of his race,

With the honey-voiced woman who beckons, and stands,

And gleams like a Dream in his face—
Like a marvelous Dream in his face?

部落灭亡时

他蜷缩着，脸深埋在膝盖上，
　　藏在他的黑发里面；
风暴摧残的树木他无法仰望，
　　想不到那里的孤独——
　　想不到那失落和孤独。

大袋鼠们在草丛间摸索，
　　因为害怕向掩体逃；
他坐在灰烬中，袋鼠身旁过
　　那里沉睡矛与回旋镖——
　　沟壑、投石机还有长矛。

呜噜啦，看他！在那岩石之顶
　　雷电伴着雨水劈开，
还有吹起那湖面盐粒的狂风，
　　使他再次成为猎手——
　　再次成为渔夫猎手。

他的双眼充满着郁积的沉思；
　　但他梦到远古狩猎，

梦到被追的敌人、经历的战斗
　　他们已经不再战斗——
　　他们已经不再去战斗。

山里的水在翻滚着充满着
　　呻吟着呻吟着向前；
有回声从山腰处传来，
　　他开始唱美妙的歌曲——
　　开始唱出美妙的歌曲。

透过四处飘散的雾隙，他看见，
　　冷酷好战的部落狂欢，
以及坐在圆木上的部落女人，
　　似吊唁者旁观，为他：
　　似母亲兼吊唁者，为他。

他会在梦中离开这荒凉地吗，
　　像酋长，回到他的部落，
回到甜美歌声召唤他的女人，
　　他的脸上如梦闪烁——
　　脸上像有着奇梦闪烁？

In Memoriam

At rest! Hard by the margin of that sea
Whose sounds are mingled with his noble verse
Now lies the shell that never more will house
The fine, strong spirit of my gifted friend.
Yea, he who flashed upon us suddenly,
A shining soul with syllables of fire,
Who sang the first great songs these lands can claim
To be their own; the one who did not seem
To know what royal place awaited him
Within the Temple of the Beautiful,
Has passed away; and we who knew him sit
Aghast in darkness, dumb with that great grief,
Whose stature yet we cannot comprehend;
While over yonder churchyard, hearsed with pines
The night-wind sings its immemorial hymn,
And sobs above a newly-covered grave.

The bard, the scholar, and the man who lived
That frank, that open-hearted life which keeps
The splendid fire of English chivalry
From dying out; the one who never wronged
A fellow-man; the faithful friend who judged

The many, anxious to be loved of him,
By what he saw, and not by what he heard,
As lesser spirits do; the brave great soul
That never told a lie or turned aside
To fly from danger; he, I say, was one
Of that bright company this sin-stained world
Can ill afford to lose.

They did not know
The hundreds who had read his sturdy verse,
And revelled over ringing major notes
The mournful meaning of the undersong
Which runs through all he wrote, and often takes
The deep autumnal, half-prophetic tone
Of forest winds in March; nor did they think
That on that healthy-hearted man there lay
The wild specific curse which seems to cling
For ever to the Poet's twofold life!

To Adam Lindsay Gordon, I who laid
Two years ago on Lionel Michael's grave
A tender leaf of my regard; yea I,
Who culled a garland from the flowers of song
To place where Harpur sleeps; I, left alone,
The sad disciple of a shining band

Now gone! To Adam Lindsay Gordon's name

I dedicate these lines; and if 'tis true

That, past the darkness of the grave, the soul

Becomes omniscient then the bard may stoop

From his high seat to take the offering,

And read it with a sigh for human friends,

In human bonds, and gray with human griefs.

And having wove and proffered this poor wreath,

I stand to-day as lone as he who saw

At nightfall through the glimmering moony mists,

The last of Arthur on the wailing mere

And strained in vain to hear the going voice.

缅怀诗人

安息吧！在那片海的边缘

波涛声和着高贵的诗文

此刻安卧的躯壳失去了

天才朋友优雅、强大灵魂。

是啊！他突然闪现在面前，

那火热音节的闪亮灵魂，

最早唱出属于这片土地

伟大的歌；他似乎不知道

在那美丽无比的殿堂里

他可以拥有高贵的一席，
他逝去了；知道他的人们
静坐在黑暗里惊恐、哀痛，
我们还不理解他的地位；
远处的墓园，埋葬在松林
夜风吟唱着远古的颂歌，
在新覆盖的坟墓上啜泣。

他是诗人、学者，一生坦率
胸怀宽广，传承英国骑士
精神的辉煌香火绝对不会
泯灭；他从不曾错待一个
友人；对那些渴望得到他
爱戴的人，他是忠诚朋友，
待人以所见，而不以所闻，
精灵般勇敢伟大的灵魂
他从不说谎，不躲避危险；
我说，他，是一位光明伙伴
这罪恶的世界无法承受
失去他的后果。

那些读过
他坚定诗行的千百万人，
陶醉于那响亮的主旋律

不知那些贯穿他作品的
隐隐伤情，常伴着三月里
森林风那深秋里半预言
式的调子；他们不曾想过
那健康心态的诗人身上
有摆脱不了的狂野诅咒
一直附着他双重的生活。

两年前，林奈·迈克尔墓地
我为亚当·林赛·戈登献上
一片嫩叶表达敬意；是的，
我将歌之花编成花环放在
哈普长眠处；我，独自留下，
那个耀眼乐队伤心学徒
不再！我在亚当·戈登墓前
献上这些诗句；如果经过
黑暗的墓地的灵魂，确实
无所不知，那诗人兴许会
从高座上屈身接纳祭献，
为仍为世俗哀伤束缚的，
在世的友人叹息地诵读。

编好花环完成祭献之后，
我孤独站着如他生前般

目睹夜幕穿过朦胧月光，
雾霭悄至时亚瑟王默默
在哭湖边听离去的歌声。

The Muse of Australia

Where the pines with the eagles are nestled in rifts,
And the torrent leaps down to the surges,
I have followed her, clambering over the cliffs,
By the chasms and moon-haunted verges.
I know she is fair as the angels are fair,
For have I not caught a faint glimpse of her there;
A glimpse of her face and her glittering hair,
And a hand with the Harp of Australia?

I never can reach you, to hear the sweet voice
So full with the music of fountains!
Oh! When will you meet with that soul of your choice
Who will lead you down here from the mountains?
A lyre-bird lit on a shimmering space;
It dazzled mine eyes and I turned from the place,
And wept in the dark for a glorious face,
And a hand with the Harp of Australia!

澳国缪斯女神

劲松和雄鹰在裂缝之间栖息，
此处更有激流汹涌而下，
我跟随她，艰难爬过悬崖峭壁，
来到月色下的峡谷绿地。
我知道她美丽如天使一般，
是否因我瞥见了她的容颜；
闪闪发光的发丝，俏丽的脸，
手在轻拨澳国竖琴琴弦？

我够不到你，也无法倾听
那溪流之声甜美满满！
哦！你何时与你选中的灵魂
相遇让他带你冲下山涧？
琴鸟暗中发出光芒耀眼；
令我目眩而不得不把身转，
暗中哭泣，为你灿烂俏脸，
手在拨动澳国竖琴琴弦！

Bell-Birds

By channels of coolness the echoes are calling,
And down the dim gorges I hear the creek falling;
It lives in the mountain, where moss and the sedges
Touch with their beauty the banks and the ledges;
Through breaks of the cedar and sycamore bowers
Struggles the light that is love to the flowers.
And, softer than slumber, and sweeter than singing,
The notes of the bell-birds are running and ringing.

The silver-voiced bell-birds, the darlings of day-time,
They sing in September their songs of the May-time.
When shadows wax strong, and the thunder-bolts hurtle,
They hide with their fear in the leaves of the myrtle;
When rain and the sunbeams shine mingle together
They start up like fairies that follow fair weather,
And straightway the hues of their feathers unfolden
Are the green and the purple, the blue and the golden.

October, the maiden of bright yellow tresses,
Loiters for love in these cool wildernesses:
Loiters knee-deep in the grasses to listen,
Where dripping rocks gleam and the leafy pools glisten.

Then is the time when the water-moons splendid
Break with their gold, and are scattered or blended
Over the creeks, till the woodlands have warning
Of songs of the bell-bird and wings of the morning.

Welcome as waters unkissed by the summers
Are the voices of bell-birds to thirsty far-comers.
When fiery December sets foot in the forest,
And the need of the wayfarer presses the sorest,
Pent in the ridges for ever and ever,
The bell-birds direct him to spring and to river,
With ring and with ripple, like runnels whose torrents
Are toned by the pebbles and leaves in the currents.

Often I sit, looking back to a childhood
Mixt with the sights and the sounds of the wildwood,
Longing for power and the sweetness to fashion
Lyrics with beats like the heart-beats of passion—
Songs interwoven of lights and of laughters
Borrowed from bell-birds in far forest rafters;
So I might keep in the city and alleys
The beauty and strength of the deep mountain valleys,
Charming to slumber the pain of my losses
With glimpses of creeks and a vision of mosses.

铃鸟

阴凉的河道回荡着阵阵鸟鸣，
幽暗峡谷间我聆听溪流叮咚；
它栖息山中，那里莎草与苔藓
轻柔地触摸着岩石与河岸；
透过雪松和梧桐树枝的缝隙
阳光艰难地爱抚着花蕊。
而且，比酣睡更柔、比歌声更甜，
那铃鸟的鸣声犹如铃声传遍。

铃鸟声如银铃，是白日的宠儿，
它们在九月唱着五月的欢歌。
每当天色渐暗，雷鸣夹着电闪，
它们害怕地躲在爱神树叶间；
当细雨与阳光交织在一起时
好似晴天精灵它们展翅飞起，
羽毛舒展霎时变得五彩斑斓
是绿色是紫色，是金色是深蓝。

十月，有个亮黄色头发的少女，
在冷清的荒野中把爱寻觅：
在齐膝的草丛中漫步聆听，
岩壁水滴闪池塘草叶亮晶晶。

这时候水中的月影荡漾着
金色光彩，时分时散时融合
于溪水之上，直到清晨林间
铃鸟的歌声和振翅之声频传。

当炎炎的夏日驻足在林中
远来口渴的客人听见铃鸟欢鸣。
如见未被烈日灼热的溪流，
徒步者已被困在山脊很久很久，
在走不完的路上苦苦寻求，
铃鸟指引他走向山泉和河流，
鸟鸣和着水声，就像河水奔驰
歌声中映衬着树叶和鹅卵石。

我常常坐着，回忆孩提光景
伴随着荒山野林的美景声音，
渴望得到创作的力量和灵气
写出激情脉动的歌词节律——
阳光与笑声交织成的歌谣
来自橡木丛林深处的铃鸟；
所以我可以在城市小巷里
留住深山峡谷的力量与美丽，
记忆中闪现的苔藓与溪流
能令我淡忘失去带来的痛苦。

Victor Daley（1858—1905）
维克多·戴利诗三首

Dreams

I have been dreaming all a summer day
Of rare and dainty poems I would write;
Love-lyrics delicate as lilac-scent,
Soft idylls woven of wind, and flower, and stream,
And songs and sonnets carven in fine gold.

The day is fading and the dusk is cold;
Out of the skies has gone the opal gleam,
Out of my heart has passed the high intent
Into the shadow of the falling night—
Must all my dreams in darkness pass away?

I have been dreaming all a summer day:

Shall I go dreaming so until Life's light

Fades in Death's dusk, and all my days are spent?

Ah, what am I the dreamer but a dream!

The day is fading and the dusk is cold.

My songs and sonnets carven in fine gold

Have faded from me with the last day-beam

That purple luster to the sea-line lent,

And flushed the clouds with rose and chrysolite,

So days and dreams in darkness pass away.

I have been dreaming all a summer day

Of songs and sonnets carven in fine gold;

But all my dreams in darkness pass away;

The day is fading, and the dusk is cold.

梦

某个夏天我整天在做梦

要写些珍奇优美的诗歌；

像丁香花般精致的情歌，

由风、花、水织就的轻柔田园诗，

纯金刻的歌和十四行诗。

天空渐暗，而黄昏也渐冷；
猫眼石光芒从空中消失，
我的梦想已从心中逝去
消失在夜幕的阴影之中——
黑暗中的梦必须消逝吗？

某个夏天我整天在做梦：
我是否该一直做梦直到
生命之光消逝，人生终结？
啊，我只不过是一个梦者！
天空渐暗，而黄昏也渐冷。

纯金刻的歌和十四行诗
随着最后一缕阳光消失
紫色的光泽留给了海面，
玫瑰和黄碧玺冲走云层，
白日和黑暗中的梦消逝。

某个夏天我整天在做梦
梦到金刻的歌、十四行诗；
但黑暗中的梦都已消逝；
天空渐暗，而黄昏也渐冷。

Tall Hat

Who rules the world with iron rod?
The person in the Tall Silk Hat.
He is its sordid lord and god—
Self-centered in a Shrine of Fat.

He keeps the Hoi Polloi in peace,
With opiates of Kingdom Come:
His is the Glory that is Grease,
The Grandeur that is Rum.

He sends the nations forth to fight,
The war-ships grim across the foam:
They battle for the right—his right—
A mortgage over hearth and home.

高帽

谁用铁棒统治世界？
戴着丝绸高帽的人。
他是卑鄙的主和神——
利益至上唯我独尊。

用来自末日的鸦片，
去控制着普通民众：
他的荣耀来自羊毛，
宏伟来自朗姆。

各国被他派去战斗，
战舰艰难跨越泡沫：
只为他的权利——而战——
牺牲了温暖的家园。

Lachesis

Over a slow-dying fire,
Dreaming old dreams, I am sitting;
The flames leap up and expire;
A woman sits opposite knitting.

I've taken a Fate to wife;
She knits with a half-smile mocking
Me, and my dreams, and my life,
All into a worsted stocking.

算命者

炉火在渐渐地熄灭，
我静坐着，做着旧梦；
火焰跳跃终熄灭；
编织的女人坐在对面。

我为妻子算命运；
她嘲笑着织着衣袜
我，梦想，我的一生，
全织进一只精纺袜。

Mary Gilmore（1865—1962）
玛丽·吉尔摩诗十首

Eve Song

The fog comes
I span and Eve span
A thread to bind the heart of man;
But the heart of man was a wandering thing
That came and went with little to bring:
Nothing he minded what we made,
As here he loitered, and there he stayed.

I span and Eve span
A thread to bind the heart of man;
But the more we span the more we found
It wasn't his heart but ours we bound.
For children gathered about our knees:
The thread was a chain that stole our ease.

And one of us learned in our children's eyes
That more than man was love and prize.
But deep in the heart of one of us lay
A root of loss and hidden dismay.

He said he was strong. He had no strength
But that which comes of breadth and length.
He said he was fond. But his fondness proved
The flame of an hour when he was moved.
He said he was true. His truth was but
A door that winds could open and shut.

And yet, and yet, as he came back,
Wandering in from the outward track,
We held our arms, and gave him our breast,
As a pillowing place for his head to rest.
I span and Eve span,
A thread to bind the heart of man!

夏娃

雾来了
我织夏娃纺
一线系住男人心房；
但是男人的心却漂泊不定

他来了又去留下空寂：
不在乎我们的付出，
在这儿徘徊，那里停留。

我织夏娃纺
一线系住男人心房；
但是纺得越多越领悟
仅我们的心被束缚。
因为孩子们围在膝处：
那线像链子偷走自由。
有人从孩子的眼中明白
重要的是赞赏与爱。
但是在我们的心灵深处
根植的是绝望与失落。

他说他很强大。但力量
只来自广泛的交往。
他说爱。爱却是感动瞬间
燃烧仅仅一小时的火焰。
他说他真诚。他的真诚
却是扇随意开关的门。

然而，然而，当他归来，
从外出的铁路走回来，
我们给他双臂，和胸膛，

我们让他得以枕着来休养。
我织夏娃纺，
一线系住男人心房！

Never Admit the Pain

Never admit the pain,
Bury it deep;
Only the weak complain,
Compliant is cheap.

Cover thy wound, fold down
Its curtained place;
Silence is still a crown,
Courage a grace.

绝不承认痛苦

绝不承认痛苦，
将它埋下；
弱者才会控诉，
抱怨很廉价。

掩盖伤口，遮好

受伤之处；
沉默仍是荣耀，
勇是风度。

An Aboriginal Simile

There was no stir among the trees,
No pulse in the earth,
No movement in the void;
The grass was a dry white fire.
Then in the distance rose a cloud,
And a swift rain came:
Like a woman running,
The wind in her hair.

一个关于土著的比喻

树林之内毫无动静，
大地无脉动，
虚空没有响动；
草是团干枯的白火。
在远处升起了一片云，
一场雨来临：

就像女子疾奔，
风拂过发丝。

Old Botany Bay

"I'm old
Botany Bay;
Stiff in the joints,
Little to say.

I am he
Who paved the way,
That you might walk
At your ease to-day;

I was the conscript
Sent to hell
To make in the desert
The living well;

I bore the heat,
I blazed the track—
Furrowed and bloody
Upon by back.

I split the rock;
I felled the tree:
The nation was—
Because of me!"

Old Botany Bay
Taking the sun
From day to day...
Shame on the mouth
That would deny
The knotted hands
That set us high!

老博塔尼湾

"我是老
博塔尼湾；
关节僵硬，
已失语。

是我曾
铺就道路，
今你才可
悠闲地漫步；

被征入地狱
的士兵
我在沙漠创造
美好生活；

忍着酷热，
开辟道路——
风霜与血汗
布满背脊。

劈开岩石；
砍倒树木：
整个国家
全都靠我！"

老博塔尼湾
沐浴阳光
日复一日……
勤劳双手
创造荣耀
谁敢鄙夷
无耻之极！

An Allegory

The fight was over, and the battle won
A soldier, who beneath his chieftain's eye
Had done a mighty deed and done it well,
And done it as the world will have it done—
A stab, a curse, some quick play of the butt,
Two skulls cracked crosswise, but the colours saved—
Proud of his wounds, proud of the promised cross,
Turned to his rear-rank man, who on his gun
Leant heavily apart. "Ho, friend!" he called,
"You did not fight then: Were you left behind?
I saw you not." The other turned and showed
A gaping, red-lipped wound upon his breast.
"Ah," said he sadly, "I was in the smoke!"
Threw up his arms, shivered, and fell and died.

这是个讽喻

战斗结束了，赢得了胜利
一士兵，在首长眼皮底下
做了一件伟大漂亮的事，
这满足了所有人的意愿——
刀刺，咒骂，屁股上的一弹，

两颗头颅撞破，血液四溅——
他为十字形的伤口，骄傲，
他转向后列的士兵，后者
重靠在枪上。"嗬，朋友！"他说，
"你没有参战：你落后了吗？
没看到你。"后者转身露出
胸前开裂的、红色的伤口。
"啊，"他伤心道，"我在硝烟里！"
举起双臂，颤抖，倒下死去。

Nationality

I have grown past hate and bitterness,
I see the world as one;
But though I can no longer hate,
My son is still my son.

All men at God's round table sit,
And all men must be fed;
But this loaf in my hand,
This loaf is my son's bread.

我们是同宗

我终放下仇恨与痛苦，
我视天下为一；
尽管我已不再仇恨，
我子仍是我子。

围坐在神的圆桌旁，
人人皆应饱食；
然而我手中的，
应是我儿之食。

The Tenancy

I shall go as my father went,
A thousand plans in his mind,
With something still held unspent,
When death let fall the blind.

I shall go as my mother went,
The ink still wet on the line;
I shall pay no rust as rent,
For the house that is mine.

房主承租

我应行事如父亲般，
对于手中的财务，
他总有万般打算，
否则终有失误。

我应行事如母亲般，
合同上墨迹仍在；
不应我支付房租，
因为我是房主。

Heritage

Not of ourselves are we free,
Not of ourselves are we strong;
The fruit is never the tree,
Nor the singer the song.

Out of temptation old, so old
The story hides in the dark untold,
In some far, dim, ancestral hour
There is our root of power.

The strength we give is the strength we make;

And the strength we have is the strength we take,

Given us down from the long-gone years,

Cleansed in the salt of others' tears.

The fruit is never the tree,

Nor the singer the song;

Not of ourselves are we free,

Not of ourselves are we strong.

代代相传

不是因自己而自由,

不是因自己而强壮;

果实不等同于树,

歌手并非歌曲。

出于古老诱惑,古老

黑暗的历史不为人道,

遥远、暗淡、古老时期

是我们力量之始。

出击的力量我们创造;

占有的力量由我们获取,

传承自那古老的岁月，
在他人泪中变纯净。

果实不等同于树，
歌手并非歌曲；
不是因自己而自由，
不是因自己而强壮。

The Myall in Prison

Lone, Lone, and lone I stand,
With none to hear my cry,
As the black feet of the night
Go walking down the sky.

The stars they seem but dust
Under those passing feet,
As they, for an instant's space,
Flicker and flame, and fleet.

So, on my heart, my grief
Hangs with the weight of doom,
And the black feet of its night
Go walking through my room.

监狱的相思树

茕、茕、孑立的我,
我哭泣无人管,
夜的黑色的脚印
正漫步到天边。

不是星光却是
脚步扬起尘泥,
因为脚下,一瞬间,
红光闪烁,消逝。

然,我内心,悲切
我与厄运同步,
而夜的黑色脚印
穿过我的囚屋。

Fourteen Men

Fourteen men,
And each hung down
Straight as a log
From his toes to his crown.

Honest poor men,
But the diggers said "Nay"!
So they strung them all up
On a fine summer's day.

There they were hanging
As we drove by,
Grown-ups on the front seat,
On the back seat I.

That was Lambing Flat,
And still I can see
The straight up and down
Of each on his tree.

十四人

十四人，
一个不落
笔直如树
个个头脚倒挂。

淳朴劳工，
但淘金者说"不"!

就在晴朗夏日
将他们吊上树。

开车经过时
我们目睹，
前排坐着大人，
后排坐着我。

那是蓝滨滩，
如今我犹记
每棵树上的
笔直的身体。

Henry Lawson（1867—1922）
亨利·劳森诗二首

Middleton's Rouseabout

Tall and freckled and sandy,
Face of a country lout;
This was the picture of Andy,
Middleton's Rouseabout.

Type of a coming nation,
In the land of cattle and sheep,
Worked on Middleton's station,
Pound a week and his keep.

On Middleton's wide dominions
Plied the stockwhip and shears;
Hadn't any opinions,
Hadn't any "ideas".

Swiftly the years went over,
Liquor and drought prevailed;
Middleton went as a drover
After his station had failed.

Type of a careless nation,
Men who are soon played out,
Middleton was: —and his station
Was bought by the Rouseabout.

Flourishing beard and sandy,
Tall and solid and stout:
This is the picture of Andy,
Middleton's Rouseabout.

Now on his own dominions
Works with his overseers;
Hasn't any opinions,
Hasn't any "ideas".

米德尔顿杂役

大高个沙色雀斑，
乡巴佬的脸皮；

这是张安迪的照片，
米德尔顿杂役。

在一个新型国度，
到处遍布着牛和羊，
为米德尔顿工作， ①
一周留下一镑。

米德尔顿领地宽广，
鞭子剪刀交替；
不曾有何念想，
也无任何"建议"。

时光就这样地消散，
酒和干旱盛行；
牧场经营不善后
米德尔顿成了牧人。

一个粗心的国度，
人们很快失败，
米德尔顿——及其牧区
被杂役安迪买进。

---

①本书采用"字数相等译法"，也就是一个英语音节用一个汉字译出。这里
原文为六个音节，因是地名无法省略，所以译文为七个字。——编者注

沙色皮肤和浓须，
高大粗壮结实：
照片里的人是安迪，
米德尔顿杂役。

现在他的领土上
与工头共劳役；
没有任何的念想，
也无任何"建议"。

Ned's Delicate Way

Ned knew I was short of tobacco one day,
And that I was too proud to ask for it;
He hated such pride, but his delicate way
Forbade him to take me to task for it.

I loathed to be cadging tobacco from Ned,
But, when I was just on the brink of it:
"I've got a new brand of tobacco," he said—
"Try a smoke, and let's know what you think of it."

内德的文雅

某日内德知道我缺少烟草，
因为骄傲我却没有索要；
他对此不喜，但文雅的风貌
令他无法对我有何指责。

我不情愿向内德讨要烟草，
但有一天，我正打算讨要：
"我有新牌子的烟草，"他说道——
"来尝尝，再告诉我它好不好。"

Christopher Brennan（1870—1932）
克里斯托弗·布伦南诗十四首

Because She Would Ask Me Why I Loved Her

If questioning could make us wise
No eyes would ever gaze in eyes;
If all our tale were told in speech
No mouths would wander each to each.

Were spirits free from mortal mesh
And love not bound in hearts of flesh
No aching breasts would yearn to meet
And find their ecstasy complete.

For who is there that lives and knows
The secret powers by which he grows?
Were knowledge all, what were our need
To thrill and faint and sweetly bleed?

Then seek not, sweet, the If and Why
I love you now until I die:
For I must love because I live
And life in me is what you give.

因她会问我为什么爱她

若提问能令人明智
就无须用眼睛凝视；
若言语能讲清缘由
不需口舌次次陈述。

灵魂不受生死束缚
爱情不由人心约束
痛苦的心渴望相见
终至欢喜不再缺憾。

活着的人是否知悉
使他成长的神秘之力？
是否明白，我们为何
激动眩晕甜蜜流血？

亲爱的，莫再问，因果
我会爱你直至死去：

我必爱因为我活着
我的生命由你给予。

How Old Is My Heart, How Old?

How old is my heart, how old, how old is my heart,
and did I ever go forth with song when the morn was new?
I seem to have trod on many ways: I seem to have left
I know not how many homes; and to leave each
was still to leave a portion of mine own heart,
of my old heart whose life I had spent to make that home
and all I had was regret, and a memory.

So I sit and muse in this wayside harbour and wait
till I hear the gathering cry of the ancient winds and again
I must up and out and leave the members of the hearth
to crumble silently into white ash and dust,
and see the road stretch bare and pale before me: again
my garment and my house shall be the enveloping winds
and my heart be fill'd wholly with their old pitiless cry.

我心有多老，多老？

我心有多老，多老，我心有多老，

当新的一日来临时，有没有哼着歌？
我似乎一直疲于奔波：我好像走过
数不清的家园；每次的离去
都意味着我心一角的遗失，
那颗心曾为建设家园操劳不已
现在剩下的只有悔恨，和记忆。

我坐在我的港湾里静静等待着
那古老的风一声声有力的呼唤；于是我
起身离去，只剩下我身后的家园
默默地化作灰白尘烟消散，
而我则凝视前方苍白荒芜之路：
我的衣物和房屋将被风悉数卷去
我苍老的心只听见那无情的呼唤。

I Saw My Life as Whitest Flame

I saw my life as whitest flame
light-leaping in a crystal sky,
and virgin colour where it came
pass'd to its heart, in love to die.
It wrapped the world in tender harm
rose-flower'd with one ecstatic pang:
God walk'd amid the hush'd alarm,

and all the trembling region rang
music, whose silver veils dispart
around the carven silences
Memnonian in the hidden heart—
now blithe, effulgurant majesties.

生命是纯白的火焰

生命是纯白的火焰
在清净空气中飞起，
它带着原有色直抵
心深处，于爱中熄灭。
它用温柔裹着伤害
瑰色喜悦伪装着悲哀：
无声警报中神走动，
在所有颤抖的区域
响起音乐，银色面纱
渗透的寂静中散开
门农深藏在我心底——
是无忧的、尊贵的大帝。

Under a Sky of Uncreated Mud

Under a sky of uncreated mud

or sunk beneath the accursed streets, my life
is added up of cupboard-musty weeks
and ring'd about with walls of ugliness:
some narrow world of ever-streaming air.
My days of azure have forgotten me.
Nought stirs, in garret-chambers of my brain,
except the squirming brood of miseries
older than memory, while, far out of sight
behind the dun blind of the rain, my dreams
of sun on leaves and waters drip thro' years
nor stir the slumbers of some sullen well,
beneath whose corpse-fed weeds I too shall sink.

在泥泞不堪的天空之下

在泥泞不堪的天空之下
被诅咒的道路之底，生活
日复一日地被发霉橱柜
和丑陋的墙壁四周环绕：
是空气流动的狭窄世界。
天蓝色日子已把我忘记。
我心之深处，无丝毫波动，
除了痛苦的不停歇蠕动
它比记忆久远，又在，视线外
的雨帘后，我梦想着阳光

浸透岁月歇于树叶水滴
却不会打搅沉睡的深井，
我将在井下腐草中沉沦。

Spring Breezes

Spring breezes over the blue,
now lightly frolicking in some tropic bay,
go forth to meet her way,
for here the spell hath won and dream is true.

O happy wind, thou that in her warm hair
mayst rest and play!
Could I but breathe all longing into thee,
so were thy viewless wing
as flame or thought, hastening her shining way.

And now I bid thee bring
tenderly hither over a subject sea
that golden one whose grace hath made me king,
and, soon to glad my gaze at shut of day,
loosen'd in happy air
her charmed hair.

春风拂

春风拂过那蔚蓝，
在热带海湾上方轻轻嬉戏，
奔向她的前路，
此刻，咒语实现，梦想成真。

啊快乐的风，她温暖发间
休憩嬉戏！
我向你倾吐所有的渴望，
你无形的翅膀
是火是思想，驱赶她的光芒。

现在我命你用
温柔之力在平静海上带来
金色光之恩典赋我王权，
不久，我快乐地凝视落日，
快乐风中松开
其美发。

An Hour's Respite

An hour's respite; once more the heart may dream:

the thunderwheels of passion thro' the eve,

distantly musical, vaporously agleam,

about my old pain leave

nought but a soft enchantment, vesper fable.

Sweet hour of dream! From the tense height of life

given back to this dear grass and perfumed shade,

across the golden darkness

I feel the simple flowerets where we stray'd

in the clear eves unmix'd with starry strife.

Ah! Wilt thou not even now arise,

low-laughing child haunting my old spring ways

and blossom freshly on my freshen'd gaze,

sororal in this hour of tenderness,

an hour of happy hands and clinging eyes—

on silent heartstrings

sweet memory fades in sweet forgetfulness.

短暂的休息

短暂休息；心可再次梦想：

激情的雷轮穿过了日暮，

远远传来乐声，和朦胧的闪光，

旧伤痕留下的

是柔和的魅力，晚祷的寓言。

梦的甜蜜！在此紧张时刻

回到迷人小草和芳香树荫，
穿过金色的黑暗
我触摸到迷路那夜的小花
那个晴朗夜晚，璀璨星光。
啊！你竟然仍然在盛开，
春天路上萦绕孩童欢笑
和放眼可见绽放的小花，
在温柔短暂时刻再次出现，
快乐的牵手和依恋的眼光——
沉默的心弦
甜蜜的记忆在甜意中消亡。

Come Out, Come Out

Come out, come out, ye souls that serve, why will ye die?
Or will ye sit and stifle in your prison-homes
dreaming of some master that holds the winds in leash
and the waves of darkness yonder in the gaunt hollow of night?
Nay, there is none that rules: all is a strife of the winds
and the night shall billow in storm full oft ere all be done.
For this is the hard doom that is laid on all of you,
to be that whereof ye dream, dreaming against your will.
But first ye must travel the many ways, and your close-wrapt souls
must be blown thro' with the rain that comes from the homeless dark:

for until ye have had care of the wastes there shall be no truce

for them nor you, nor home, but ever the ancient feud;

and the soul of man must house the cry of the darkling waves

as he follows the ridge above the waters shuddering to-wards night,

and the rains and the winds that roam anhunger'd for some heart's
　　warmth.

Go: tho' ye find it bitter, yet must ye be bare

to the wind and the sea and the night and the wail of birds in the sky;

go: tho' the going be hard and the goal blinded with rain

yet the staying is a death that is never soften'd with sleep.

出来，出来

出来，出来，苦难灵魂，为何要死？

难道你愿意在牢狱中窒息

梦里自由的风被主宰被禁锢

黑暗如浪潮在空寂夜空中汹涌肆虐？

不，不该被主宰：都只是风的斗争

黑夜将在暴风中翻滚又最终退却。

这就是强加于你们身上的劫数，

你梦中所见，却与你的意愿背驰。

但是你必须先走过许多路，被束缚的

灵魂必须穿过无边黑暗中的风雨：

除非你能改变，否则无法为他们，你们

或家园，等来休战，争端自古不断；

而灵魂必须经受暗黑浪涌的嘶吼
他才能沿着水中之路颤抖着走入那黑暗，
风与雨渴望吞噬掉人心深处的温暖。
去吧：尽管前路艰难，仍无畏惧
那风那雨那海那夜还有空中鸟儿的啸叫；
去吧：尽管前路漫漫雨水挡住视线
然而留下面对的死亡威胁永不消散。

My Heart Was Wandering in the Sands

My heart was wandering in the sands,
a restless thing, a scorn apart;
love set his fire in my hands,
I clasp'd the flame unto my heart.

Surely, I said, my heart shall turn
one fierce delight of pointed flame;
and in that holocaust shall burn
its old unrest and scorn and shame:

Surely my heart the heavens at last
shall storm with fiery orisons,
and know, enthroned in the vast,
the fervid peace of molten suns.

The flame that feeds upon my heart
fades or flares, by wild winds controll'd;
my heart still walks a thing apart,
my heart is restless as of old.

我的心在沙滩上徘徊

我的心在沙滩上徘徊，
焦躁不安，破碎不堪；
我手中燃烧着爱，
我将火焰捧至心田。

我说，当然，是我的心
因那火舌变得狂喜；
爱火熊熊燃烧燃尽
那羞惭与不安轻蔑：

我心最终会进入天堂
鸣响起炽热的祈祷，
在广阔的平原上，
感受烈日下的平和。

我心上燃烧的火焰

或明或灭，由风评判；
我心依然破碎不堪，
我心依旧焦躁不安。

The Winter Eve Is Clear and Chill

The winter eve is clear and chill:
the world of air is folded still;
the quiet hour expects the moon;
and yon my home awaits me soon
behind the panes that come and go
with dusk and firelight wavering low:
and I must bid the prompting cease
that bids me, in this charmed peace,
—as tho' the hour would last my will—
follow the roads and follow still
the dream that holds my heart in trance
and lures it to the fabled chance
to find, beyond these evening ways,
the morning and the woodland days
and meadows clear with gold, and you
as once, ere I might dare to woo.

冬夜晴朗而且寒冷

冬夜晴朗而且寒冷：
空气世界静默无声；
安静时刻盼着月起；
家人在盼着我的归期
暮色沉沉却见窗内
隐约透出炉火的摇曳：
我须按捺归心似箭
此刻，迷人的夜晚，
——似将持续我的愿望——
继续行进跟从梦想
那梦令我寤寐思服
它使我心恍然领悟
在那夜色沉沉之后，
是黎明是林地白昼
是金色牧场，还有你
我将，吐露我的爱意。

Romance

Of old, on her terrace at evening
... not here... in some long-gone kingdom

O, folded close to her breast! ...

—Our gaze dwelt wide on the blackness
(Was it trees? Or a shadowy passion
the pain of an old-world longing
that it sobb'd, that it swell'd, that it shrank?)
—the gloom of the forest
blurr'd soft on the skirt of the night-skies
that shut in our lonely world.

... Not here... in some long-gone world...

Close-lock'd in that passionate arm-clasp
no word did we utter, we stirr'd not:
the silence of Death, or of Love...
only, round and over us
that tearless infinite yearning
and the Night with her spread wings rustling
folding us with the stars.

... Not here... in some long-gone kingdom
of old, on her terrace at evening
O, folded close to her heart! ...

浪漫

从前，傍晚在她露台上
……非此处……过去的王国
啊，紧贴她的胸膛！……

——两双眼睛注视黑暗
（是树？或阴影下的激情
旧日渴望带来痛苦
它是在哭泣、膨胀、收缩？）
——森林中的阴霾
夜空里变得模糊柔和
远离这二人世界。

……非此处……过去世界……

情意绵绵紧紧拥抱着
一句话不说，动也不动：
死般的沉默，或爱意……
围绕我们的，仅
是泪干的无限向往
那展翅作响的黑夜下
我们与星共处。

……非此处……过去的王国

从前，傍晚在她露台上

啊，紧贴她的胸膛！……

Summer Noon

Fire in the heavens, and fire along the hills,

and fire made solid in the flinty stone,

thick-massed or scattered pebble, fire that fills

the breathless hour that lives in fire alone.

This valley, long ago the patient bed

of floods that carved its ancient amplitude,

in stillness of the Egyptian crypt outspread,

endures to drown in noon-day's tyrant mood.

Behind the veil of burning silence bound,

vast life's innumerous busy littleness

is hushed in vague-conjectured blur of sound

that dulls the brain with slumbrous weight, unless

some dazzling puncture let the stridence throng

in the cicada's torture-point of song.

夏当午

天气热火炎炎，群山也热火炎炎，

火在坚硬的石头中凝固，
或多或少的鹅卵石，火热
中感受独有的窒息时刻。
山谷，很久前是洪水病床
任由水流刻下丝丝旧痕，
在埃及地穴的寂静中外延，
忍受正午暴君情绪喷发。
在火燎般的寂静面纱后，
浩瀚生命那些无数忙碌的
渺小被模糊的声音淹没
这令大脑沉沉欲睡，除非
破裂小孔爆发的刺裂声
才能搅乱这蝉鸣的折磨。

Was It the Sun That Broke My Dream?

Was it the sun that broke my dream
or was't the dazzle of thy hair
caught where our olden meadows seem
themselves again and yet more fair?
Ah, sun that woke me, limpid stream,
then in spring-mornings' rapture of air!

Was it the sun that broke my dream

or was't the dazzle of thy hair?

And didst not thou beside me gleam,

brought hither by a tender care

at least my slumbering grief to share?

Was it the sun that broke my dream?

是太阳唤醒我的梦？

是太阳唤醒我的梦？

抑或你耀眼的金发

让我们古老的牧场

没有变样却更光鲜？

我、清溪被太阳唤醒，

啊，还有春晨欢喜氛围！

是太阳唤醒我的梦，

抑或你耀眼的金发？

你是否由柔风送来，

在我的身旁发出光芒

分摊我沉睡的悲哀？

是太阳唤醒我的梦？

I Am Shut Out of Mine Own Heart

I am shut out of mine own heart
because my love is far from me,
nor in the wonders have I part
that fill its hidden empery:

The wildwood of adventurous thought
and lands of dawn my dream had won,
the riches out of Faery brought
are buried with our bridal sun.

And I am in a narrow place,
and all its little streets are cold,
because the absence of her face
has robb'd the sullen air of gold.

My home is in a broader day:
at times I catch it glistening
thro' the dull gate, a flower'd play
and odour of undying spring:

The long days that I lived alone,
sweet madness of the springs I miss'd,

are shed beyond, and thro' them blown
clear laughter, and my lips are kiss'd:

—and here, from mine own joy apart,
I wait the turning of the key: —
I am shut out of mine own heart
because my love is far from me.

我被我心拒之门外

我被我心拒之门外
因爱已经远远离去，
不再会有任何精彩
填满隐秘王国疆域：

冒险思想的原始大树
梦里黎明时的土地，
仙境带来的财富
都埋葬于新婚之日。

而我困于方寸之地，
街道狭窄且又无意，
她的面容已经失去
夺去了金子般空气。

我家曾经占地宽阔：
偶尔透过大门看去
我见它发光熠熠，
花与香气无限春意：

独自度过漫长岁月，
错过季季盎然春意，
回顾往昔，春风拂掠
清脆笑声，红唇轻启：

——如今，快乐已被剥离，
我等待开门声再起：——
我被我心拒之门外
因爱已经远远离去。

I SAID, This Misery Must End

I SAID, This misery must end:
Shall I, that am a man and know
that sky and wind are yet my friend,
sit huddled under any blow?
so speaking left the dismal room
and stept into the mother-night
all fill'd with sacred quickening gloom

where the few stars burn'd low and bright,
and darkling on my darkling hill
heard thro' the beaches' sullen boom
heroic note of living will
rung trumpet-clear against the fight;
so stood and heard, and rais'd my eyes
erect, that they might drink of space,
and took the night upon my face,
till time and trouble fell away
and all my soul sprang up to feel
as one among the stars that reel
in rhyme on their rejoicing way,
breaking the elder dark, nor stay
but speed beyond each trammelling gyre,
till time and sorrow fall away
and night be wither'd up, and fire
consume the sickness of desire.

我说，别再继续伤悲

我说，别再继续伤悲：
难道我，知道天空与
清风是我友的男士，
应该蜷缩一团被揍？
话音渐离阴沉房间

进入茫茫夜的黑暗
黑暗之神令夜更幽暗
仅几颗星低垂微闪，
我在黑黝黝的山上
从隆隆的海水声中
听到求生音符奏响
歌颂战士们的英勇；
我站着听着，抬眼看
它们，会把一切带走，
仅留黑夜迎面扑来，
直至时间纷争消逝
我的灵魂慢慢飞升
伴着寥寥几颗星辰
欣欣然地共舞挪移，
打破亘古星空，不因
险阻减速或停下脚步，
直至时间冲走悲痛
直至夜色暗淡，直至
火舌吞噬人之恶欲。

注：mother-night 源自德国著名作家歌德的诗剧 *Faust*
（《浮士德》），是"孕育光明之黑暗"的意思。

Hugh Raymond MacRae（1876—1958）
休·雷蒙德·麦克雷诗二首

Song of the Rain

Night,
And the yellow pleasure of candle-light…
Old brown books and the kind fine face of the clock
Fogged in the veils of the fire—its cuddling stock.

The cat,
Greening her eyes on the flame-litten mat;
Wickedly wakeful she yawns at the rain
Bending the roses over the pane,
And a bird in my heart begins to sing
Over and over the same sweet thing—

Safe in the house with my boyhood's love,
And our children asleep in the attic above.

夜雨之歌

夜，
昏黄的烛光给予的安宁……
棕色的旧书和精美的钟面
烛光憧憧里朦胧——它的摇篮。

那猫，
伏在软垫上眼眸绿莹莹；
雨声中被惊醒打着哈欠
拨弄窗台上的玫瑰花，
我心中的小鸟开始欢歌
一遍遍唱颂甜美生活——

与少时爱人安于一室，
我和她的孩子们在楼上酣睡。

Winds

The wind takes colour from the trees;
Through trees the wind grows green;
And, like a blue wave from the seas,
The ocean wind is seen.

The red road paints the road-wind red,
And down the ripe gold corn
The chuckling wind with golden head
Trots merrily at morn.

The black lake gives the black wind birth,
The brown breeze blows along
The ploughed brown cocked-up smoking earth
To the tune of a hunting song.

The white wind moves in the white moon's wake,
With straight white streaming hair,
And ever she wails in words that ache
The burthen of her despair.

O gusty soul that lives within,
Why dost thou flush and fade,
Wind-like, to flame and icicle—
Red Rahab and white Maid!

风

风从树上吹来颜色；
风穿林而染绿；

就像，因那蓝色浪波，
海风蒙上蓝意。

风被红路涂成红色，
又穿过玉米地
金色的风轻声笑着
跑过快乐晨曦。

黑风出自黑色湖面，
褐色微风吹拂
犁过的农田冒轻烟
和着狩猎曲的旋律。

风在白月光初醒时刻，
拂动飘逸白发，
她用痛苦话语哭诉着
令人绝望的负担。

啊，那狂风般的灵魂，
为何这样消去，
如风，如烟消冰融——
红喇合、白少女！

Vance Palmer（1885—1958）
万斯·帕尔默诗一首

The Farmer Remembers the Somme

Will they never fade or pass!
The mud, and the misty figures endlessly coming
In file through the foul morass,
And the grey flood-water lipping the reeds and grass,
And the steel wings drumming.

The hills are bright in the sun:
There's nothing changed or marled in the well-known places;
When work for the day is done
There's talk, and quiet laughter, and gleams of fun
On the old folks' faces.

I have returned to these:
The farm, and the kindly bush, and the young calves lowing;

But all that my mind sees

Is a quaking bog in a mist—stark, snapped trees,

And the dark Somme flowing.

农夫惦记的索姆河

永不褪色或消失！

泥浆，雾中的物体无穷无尽涌来

依次穿过沼泽地，

灰色潮水拍打着野草与芦苇，

钢铁之翼敲击。

日光下山丘明亮：

这些熟悉的地方没改变丝毫；

一天的工作结束

老人们，在闲聊，无声地欢笑，

脸上快乐闪耀。

我回归到这里：

农场，温和的灌木，哞哞叫的小牛；

思绪停在雾里

沼泽——光秃秃、噼啪作响的树，

深色河水湍流。

Kenneth Slessor（1901—1971）
肯尼斯·斯莱塞诗十一首

Country Towns

Country towns, with your willows and squares,
And farmers bouncing on barrel mares
To public houses of yellow wood
With "1860" over their doors,
And that mysterious race of Hogans
Which always keeps the General Stores…

At the School of Arts, a broadsheet lies
Sprayed with the sarcasm of flies:
"The Great Golightly Family
Of Entertainers Here To-night"—
Dated a year and a half ago,
But left there, less from carelessness
Than from a wish to seem polite.

Verandas baked with musky sleep,

Mulberry faces dozing deep,

And dogs that lick the sunlight up

Like paste of gold—or, roused in vain

By far, mysterious buggy-wheels,

Lower their ears, and drowse again…

Country towns with your schooner bees,

And locusts burnt in the pepper-trees,

Drown me with syrups, arch your boughs,

Find me a bench, and let me snore,

Till, charged with ale and unconcern,

I'll think it's noon at half-past four!

小乡镇

小乡镇，有广场与柳树，

农夫骑着矮胖马颠簸

去门上标着"1860"

黄色木材造的酒馆，

还有那些神神秘秘的

霍根人经营的杂货店……

艺术学校，贴着宣传纸

布满苍蝇颇具讽刺：
"伟大的戈莱特利家
艺人今晚在此献艺"——
这是一年半前的宣传，
留着，说是出于礼貌
不如说是粗心大意。

游廊带着麝香入睡，
桑树也在打着瞌睡，
野狗在舔舐着仿佛
金浆的日光——要么，被
远处的车轮声唤醒，
垂下耳朵，再次酣睡……

小乡镇有成群蜜蜂，
辣椒树上烧死的蝗虫，
喂我甜浆，垂下枝丫，
给我长凳，让我酣眠，
直到，享美酒与无忧，
以为是下午四点半！

Five Bells

Time that is moved by little fidget wheels

Is not my Time, the flood that does not flow.
Between the double and the single bell
Of a ship's hour, between a round of bells
From the dark warship riding there below,
I have lived many lives, and this one life
Of Joe, long dead, who lives between five bells.

Deep and dissolving verticals of light
Ferry the falls of moonshine down. Five bells
Coldly rung out in a machine's voice. Night and water
Pour to one rip of darkness, the Harbour floats
In air, the Cross hangs upside-down in water.

Why do I think of you, dead man, why thieve
These profitless lodgings from the flukes of thought
Anchored in Time? You have gone from earth,
Gone even from the meaning of a name;
Yet something's there, yet something forms its lips
And hits and cries against the ports of space,
Beating their sides to make its fury heard.

Are you shouting at me, dead man, squeezing your face
In agonies of speech on speechless panes?
Cry louder, beat the windows, bawl your name!

But I hear nothing, nothing... only bells,

Five bells, the bumpkin calculus of Time.

Your echoes die, your voice is dowsed by Life,

There's not a mouth can fly the pygmy strait—

Nothing except the memory of some bones

Long shoved away, and sucked away, in mud;

And unimportant things you might have done,

Or once I thought you did; but you forgot,

And all have now forgotten—looks and words

And slops of beer; your coat with buttons off,

Your gaunt chin and pricked eye, and raging tales

Of Irish kings and English perfidy,

And dirtier perfidy of publicans

Groaning to God from Darlinghurst.

Five bells.

Then I saw the road, I heard the thunder

Tumble, and felt the talons of the rain

The night we came to Moorebank in slab-dark,

So dark you bore no body, had no face,

But a sheer voice that rattled out of air

(As now you'd cry if I could break the glass),

A voice that spoke beside me in the bush,

Loud for a breath or bitten off by wind,

Of Milton, melons, and the Rights of Man,

And blowing flutes, and how Tahitian girls
Are brown and angry-tongued, and Sydney girls
Are white and angry-tongued, or so you'd found.

But all I heard was words that didn't join
So Milton became melons, melons girls,
And fifty mouths, it seemed, were out that night,
And in each tree an Ear was bending down,
Or something had just run, gone behind grass,
When, blank and bone-white, like a maniac's thought,
The naphtha-flash of lightning slit the sky,
Knifing the dark with deathly photographs.
There's not so many with so poor a purse
Or fierce a need, must fare by night like that,
Five miles in darkness on a country track,
But when you do, that's what you think.

> Five bells.

In Melbourne, your appetite had gone,
Your angers too; they had been leeched away
By the soft archery of summer rains
And the sponge-paws of wetness, the slow damp
That stuck the leaves of living, snailed the mind,
And showed your bones, that had been sharp with rage,
The sodden ecstasies of rectitude.

I thought of what you'd written in faint ink,

Your journal with the sawn-off lock, that stayed behind

With other things you left, all without use,

All without meaning now, except a sign

That someone had been living who now was dead:

"At Labassa. Room 6x8

On top of the tower; because of this, very dark

And cold in winter. Everything has been stowed

Into this room—500 books all shapes

And colours, dealt across the floor

And over sills and on the laps of chairs;

Guns, photos of many different things

And different curioes that I obtained..."

In Sydney, by the spent aquarium-flare

Of penny gaslight on pink wallpaper,

We argued about blowing up the world,

But you were living backward, so each night

You crept a moment closer to the breast,

And they were living, all of them, those frames

And shapes of flesh that had perplexed your youth,

And most your father, the old man gone blind,

With fingers always round a fiddle's neck,

That graveyard mason whose fair monuments

And tablets cut with dreams of piety

Rest on the bosoms of a thousand men
Staked bone by bone, in quiet astonishment
At cargoes they had never thought to bear,
These funeral-cakes of sweet and sculptured stone.

Where have you gone? The tide is over you,
The turn of midnight water's over you,
As Time is over you, and mystery,
And memory, the flood that does not flow.
You have no suburb, like those easier dead
In private berths of dissolution laid—
The tide goes over, the waves ride over you
And let their shadows down like shining hair,
But they are Water; and the sea-pinks bend
Like lilies in your teeth, but they are Weed;
And you are only part of an Idea.
I felt the wet push its black thumb-balls in,
The night you died, I felt your eardrums crack,
And the short agony, the longer dream,
The Nothing that was neither long nor short;
But I was bound, and could not go that way,
But I was blind, and could not feel your hand.
If I could find an answer, could only find
Your meaning, or could say why you were here
Who now are gone, what purpose gave you breath

Or seized it back, might I not hear your voice?

I looked out of my window in the dark
At waves with diamond quills and combs of light
That arched their mackerel-backs and smacked the sand
In the moon's drench, that straight enormous glaze,
And ships far off asleep, and Harbour-buoys
Tossing their fireballs wearily each to each,
And tried to hear your voice, but all I heard
Was a boat's whistle, and the scraping squeal
Of seabirds' voices far away, and bells,
Five bells. Five bells coldly ringing out.

　　　　　　　　　　　　　　　　　Five bells.

五声

小小机轮不停地推动的
不是我的时间，而是死水。
轮船上不时传来一两声
钟响，停泊于堤下的战舰
昏暗之中发出一阵钟声，
我几经生死时刻，在五次
钟声间，回顾乔，短暂一生。

月光如瀑布水垂直而下，

发着幽深消融的光。五次
钟声发自无情冰冷。夜色与潮水
涌进黑暗的裂缝，海港在空
气中飘移，十字架倒映水中。

为何会想起你，逝者，为何
毫无意义却将时间深处的
记忆钩锚拉起？你离去，
甚至带走姓名的意义；
却留下了什么，发出声音
在港湾之处撞击哭叫着，
敲打着堤坝，发泄着怒气。

逝者，你向我叫喊，脸挤压沉默
窗玻璃倾诉着你的苦难？
大哭，敲打窗，喊出你的名！

但我没听见，没有……仅钟声，
五声响，按乡下时间演算。
你的声被生活消去，湮灭，
它不能飞越这狭窄海峡——
除了那些经久被浪远推去
消散于淤泥的、尸骨的、回忆；
还有你可能做过的小事，
或我记得、你却遗忘的事，

皆已被忘记——神情和言语，
溢出的啤酒，敞开的外套，
憔悴神情和刺痛的眼，及
爱尔兰王悲剧和英王背义，
哀求上帝的达令赫斯特
政客更肮脏的背弃。

五声。

然后我看到路，听见雷鸣
感受到雨的魔爪，暗夜中
那晚我们来到了摩班克，
黑得不见你的身体，和脸，
仅轻细嗓音划过空气
（如我打碎玻璃时你哭泣），
是丛林中我耳边的轻语，
轻若一口呼吸被风吹去。
弥尔顿、瓜果、人权法案，和
笛声，还说到棕肤色的爱
发脾气的大溪地姑娘，和
肤白的悉尼姑娘，同脾气。

我只听见不连贯的词
弥尔顿听成甜瓜、瓜姑娘。
那晚说话声在四处回荡，
每棵树上似都有人窃听，

什么东西溜走，藏于草丛，
此时，闪电，犹如疯子的思想，
用苍白与骨感劈开夜空，
用死亡的图像划破黑暗。
很少有人像我这般囊中
羞涩或者渴望，这样过夜，
乡间小路上夜行五英里，
如此行事，即你所思。

　　　　　　　　　　　　　　五声。

你的脾气和怒火，消散
在墨尔本；它们都已经被
夏雨柔软箭头射中剥离
柔软的湿意、徘徊的水汽
粘住生命的叶，凝滞思维，
露出你的尸骨，你曾怒意
喷薄也曾为正直而自喜。
我想起你用淡色墨水写的
日志，锁已被锯去，和你的其他
遗物放在一起，再无用处，
更无任何意义，除了证明
有人曾在人世间走过一遭：
"在拉巴萨，6x8 房
位在塔顶上方，因而，在冬季总是
又黑又冷。似乎所有东西都

塞进此屋——500 本形形
色色的书，散落地板、
窗台还有那些椅座之上；
枪、记录不同事物的照片
和我收集的各种新鲜玩意······"

在悉尼，借着廉价煤气灯
投在粉色壁纸上的微光，
我们讨论如何炸毁世界，
但你却退缩了，每个夜晚
你都会悄悄退回至胸膛，
所有，那些活物，曾经迷惑
你青春年华的肉体之形，
尤其你的父亲，双目失明、
拿着提琴的失明的老人，
墓地石匠，他用虔诚之梦
雕刻出精致美伦的墓碑，
安放在千万人的胸膛上
在平静的惊愕中，那些尸骸
静静躺着，从不愿意承受
那些香甜祭品和精美墓石。

你在何方？潮水将你淹没，
那午夜的旋涡将你淹没，
正如同那时间，神秘，回忆

那停滞的洪流，将你淹没。
你无处安息，像那些死于
安宁的人般长眠于私域——
潮水奔腾着，浪花将你淹没
投下如亮泽秀发的波影，
却是水；海石竹在你口中
犹如百合飘摇，却是野草；
而你只是印象中的残影。
潮水将它的黑拇指推进，
死亡之夜，你的鼓膜破裂，
短暂的疼痛，长长的梦境，
和跨越时间长度的虚无；
但我注定，不能与你同行，
但我无法，握住你的双手。
如果我知晓答案，你的生命
的意义，你曾来过这世界
却又离去，是什么给予你
呼吸却又夺去，令你沉寂？

望出窗外我看见黑暗中
波涛闪烁着宝石般的光芒，
如鲭鱼拱着背脊拍打沙滩
月光，为水色镀上了釉彩，
远处酣眠的船舶，港湾处
似在相互投掷亮光的浮标，

努力捕捉你的声音，我却
只听见笛声，和远处海鸟
那刺耳的哀啼，还有钟声，
五次。冷冷的五次钟声。

五声。

Polarities

Sometimes she is like sherry, like the sun through a vessel of glass,
Like light through an oriel window in a room of yellow wood;
Sometimes she is the colour of lions, of sand in the fire of noon,
Sometimes as bruised with shadows as the afternoon.

Sometimes she moves like rivers, sometimes like trees;
Or tranced and fixed like South Pole silences;
Sometimes she is beauty, sometimes fury, sometimes neither,
Sometimes nothing drained of meaning, null as water.

Sometimes, when she makes pea-soup or plays me *Schumann*,
I love her one way; sometimes I love her another
More disturbing way when she opens her mouth in the dark;
Sometimes I like her with camellias, sometimes with a parsley-stalk,
Sometimes I like her swimming in a mirror on the wall;
Sometimes I don't like her at all.

极端感情

有时她像雪莉酒，像透过玻璃杯的阳光，
也像穿过窗棂照进黄木房间的光线；
有时她是雄狮的毛色，火热正午时的沙黄色，
有时却仿佛是午后斑驳暗色。

有时她动如河流，如树木般；
或者是静似南极的寂寥；
有时她是美，是怒火，有时两者皆非，
有时如水一般无形，毫无意义。

有时，她洗手做羹或弹奏舒曼，
我爱她如此；有时我又爱她夜中
喃喃细语搅乱我宁静心弦的模样；
有时我爱她如山茶花，有时又是欧芹茎，
有时我爱墙上镜中她的灵动身影；
有时对她无动于衷。

　　注：Robert Schumann（罗伯特·舒曼，1810—1856），19
世纪德国作曲家。

To the Poetry of Hugh McCrae

Uncles who burst on childhood, from the East,
Blown from air, like bearded ghosts arriving,
And are, indeed, a kind of guessed-at ghost
Through mumbled names at dinner-tables moving,

Bearers of parrots, bonfires of blazing stones,
Their pockets fat with riches out of reason,
Meerschaum and sharks'-teeth, ropes of China coins,
And weeds and seeds and berries blowzed with poison—

So, from the baleful Kimberleys of thought,
From the mad continent of dreams, you wander,
Spending your trophies at our bloodless feet,
Mocking our fortunes with more desperate plunder;

So with your boomerangs of rhyme you come,
With blossoms wrenched from sweet and deadly branches,
And we, pale Crusoes in the moment's tomb,
Watch, turn aside, and touch again those riches,

Nor ask what beaches of the mind you trod,
What skies endured, and unimagined rivers,

Or whiteness trenched by what mysterious tide,
And aching silence of the Never-Nevers;

Watch, turn aside, and touch with easy faith
Your chest of miracles, but counting nothing,
Or dumbly, that you stole them out of death,
Out of death's pyramids, to prove us breathing.

We breathe, who beat the sides of emptiness,
We live, who die by statute in steel hearses,
We dance, whose only posture gives us grace
To squeeze the greasy udders of our purses—

(Look in this harsher glass, and I will show you
The daylight after the darkness, and the morning
After the midnight, and after the night the day
After the year after, terribly returning.)

We live by these, your masks and images,
We breathe in this, your quick and borrowed body;
But you take passage on the ruffian seas,
And you are vanished in the dark already.

献给休·麦克雷的诗歌

大叔们自东方，在我幼年，
被风吹来，似大胡子游魂，
确实的，是，在餐桌上嚷嚷
说出的可猜到其名的游魂。

鹦鹉笼子，炽热的石头篝火，
他们的口袋无故变得富有，
海泡石和鲨鱼齿，中国钱币，
有毒性的野草、种子和浆果——

所以，邪恶的金伯利思想，
在疯狂的梦想大陆，你徘徊，
我们的血是你的战利品，
无情地掠夺嘲弄我们的命脉；

所以去了又来一再出现，
甜美致命的枝上夺下花瓣，
我们，此刻墓中孤寂残骸，
注视，转身，再次触摸那财产，

不问踏过心上哪片海滩，
享用怎样的天空，怎样的河流，

洁白被怎样的神秘潮水，
和绝不要的痛苦沉默撕破；

以肤浅信仰观察，转过身
摸你的神奇宝箱，一无所获，
也许无声地，你自死亡的，
金字塔偷去，证明我们曾活着。

呼吸，我们曾击退了虚无，
活着，却在钢制灵车中死去，
跳舞，仅剩舞姿保有体面
以方便你挤榨我们的乳汁——

（看看这块粗糙的玻璃，来看
暗夜后的日光，还有午夜过后
晨曦，而后白日之后又是黑夜
一年复一年，可怕地循环往复。）

活着，靠你的面具和身影，
呼吸，在你突如其来的身体里；
而你在无情大海上远去，
已经远远地消失在黑暗里。

Winter Dawn

At five I wake, rise, rub on the smoking pane
A port to see—water breathing in the air,
Boughs broken. The sun comes up in a golden stain,
Floats like a glassy sea-fruit. There is mist everywhere,
White and humid, and the Harbour is like plated stone,
Dull flakes of ice. One light drips out alone,
One bead of winter-red, smouldering in the steam,
Quietly over the roof-tops—another window
Touched with a crystal fire in the sun's gullies,
One lonely star of the morning, where no stars gleam.

Far away on the rim of this great misty cup,
The sun gilds the dead suburbs as he rises up,
Diamonds the wind-cocks, makes glitter the crusted spikes
On moss-drowned gables. Now the tiles drip scarlet-wet,
Swim like birds' paving-stones, and sunlight strikes
Their watery mirrors with a moister rivulet,
Acid and cold. Here lie those mummied Kings,
Men sleeping in houses, embalmed in stony coffins,
Till the Last Trumpet calls their gallcries up,
And the suburbs rise with distant murmurings.

O buried dolls, O men sleeping invisible there,
I stare above your mounds of stone, lean down,
Marooned and lonely in this bitter air,
And in one moment deny your frozen town,
Renounce your bodies—earth falls in clouds away,
Stones lose their meaning, substance is lost in clay,
Roofs fade, and that small smoking forgotten heap,
The city, dissolves to a shell of bricks and paper,
Empty, without purpose, a thing not comprehended,
A broken tomb, where ghosts unknown sleep.

And the least crystal weed, shaken with frost,
The furred herbs of silver, the daisies round-eyed and tart,
Painted in antic china, the smallest night-flower tossed
Like a bright penny on the lawn, stirs more my heart,
Strikes deeper this morning air, than mortal towers
Dried to a common blindness, fainter than flowers,
Fordone, extinguished, as the vapours break,
And dead in the dawn. O Sun that kills with life,
And brings to breath all silent things—O Dawn,
Waken me with old earth, keep me awake!

冬之晨

五点醒，起身，抹去窗上雾气

就看见港口——水蒸气在翻腾，
树枝剥离。太阳升起金色尽染，
如透明海产果实飘浮。白雾弥漫，
湿意四散，海港就像镀金的石头，
哑白的冰块。一束光照落，
冬日暖色光束，在云雾中闷燃，
在静静的屋顶上——还有另一扇窗
触摸着太阳沟壑亮光之处，
无星光闪耀，仅一颗孤独晨星。

薄雾绵绵的杯形港口的远处，
初阳为沉寂的城郊镀上金边，
为风向标镶上宝石，满墙苔藓
硬刺闪闪发亮，瓦上滴滴露红，
鸟的铺路石，阳光敲击着
它们那光亮如镜泛着冷意的，
滴流。长眠室内的木乃伊，
国王们的不腐之体，陈列石棺中，
直到最后一声号角的召唤，
幽幽怨声中整个城郊苏醒。

啊，被埋的娃娃、无声无息的眠者，
我看着你们的石棺，放下，
凛冽空气中的孤单寂寒，
即刻否认冰寒村镇的存在，

还有你们的尸体——云消尘落，
石棺失去了意义，万物归尘，
屋顶消去，雾气缭绕不再见，
整个城镇，消散为石块与纸片，
虚无，一切失去目的，无法被理解，
破坟墓，无名魂灵沉睡。

脆弱的野草，风霜中颤抖，
白绒绒的圆形花朵，是迷人雏菊，
画里的古瓷瓶，插着小小的午夜花
如硬币抛在草坪上，搅乱我心，
和今晨空气，凡人世界不如它，
却是干枯暗哑，脆弱甚于花朵，
摧毁，湮灭，如泡沫般破碎，
逝于黎明。啊阳光带走生机，
又予以万物呼吸——啊黎明，
用古老大地，将我唤醒！

New Magic

At last I know—it's on old ivory jars,
Glassed with old miniatures and garnered once with musk.
I've seen those eyes like smouldering April stars
As carp might see them behind their bubbled skies

In pale green fishponds—they're as green your eyes,
As lakes themselves, changed to green stone at dusk.

At last I know—it's paned in a crystal hoop
On powder-boxes from some dead Italian girl,
I've seen such eyes grow suddenly dark, and droop
Their small, pure lids, as if I'd pried too far
In finding you snared there on that ivory jar
By crusted motes of rose and smoky-pearl.

新魔法

终于知道——它在旧象牙罐上，
像玻璃上的旧缩影，麝香气味。
看见像四月星阴郁的眼睛
如鲤鱼在苍绿的鱼塘吞吐
气泡时所见——你的双眸绿似
湖水，暮色中变成绿石。

终于知道——它在某个死去的
意大利女孩粉盒的水晶箍上，
看见这眼睛忽然暗淡，垂下
小巧、纯净的眼睑，似因我的
刺探才发现你已经被玫瑰和
烟色珍珠困在象牙罐上。

Fixed Ideas

Ranks of electroplated cubes, dwindling to glitters,
Like the other pasture, the trigonometry of marble,
Death's candy-bed. Stone caked on stone,
Dry pyramids and racks of iron balls.
Life is observed, a precipitate of pellets,
Or grammarians freeze it into spar,
Their rhomboids, as for instance, the finest crystal
Fixing a snowfall under glass. Gods are laid out
In alabaster, with horny cartilage
And zinc ribs; or systems of ecstasy
Baked into bricks. There is a gallery of sculpture,
Bleached bones of heroes, Gorgon masks of bushrangers;
But the quarries are of more use than this,
Filled with the rolling of huge granite dice,
Ideas and judgments: vivisection, the Baptist Church,
Good men and bad men, polygamy, birth-control...

Frail tinkling rush
Water-hair streaming
Prickles and glitters
Cloudy with bristles
River of thought

Swimming the pebbles—
Undo, loosen your bubbles!

老想法

一排排电镀块，渐缩小直至光亮，
既像牧场的形状，也像三角的大理石，
死亡温床。石块叠加，
干燥金字塔和铁球支架。
发现生命，就是那些球形制品，
被语法学家冻成晶石，
它们的纹理好比精美的晶体
玻璃下的雪花。摆放着用石膏
制作的神佛，带着软骨尖角
镀锌肋骨；迷人的器官是
烧制的砖块。有一家雕塑展览馆，
英雄白骨，丛林人戈耳工面具；
采石场却比它更加实用，
四处滚动的花岗岩骰子，
想法和观点：活体的解剖、浸信会、
好人与坏人、一夫多妻制、节育……

微弱水声
溪流中水草
尖刺而光亮

毛刺布满了
思想之河
流过了砾石——
松开，释放出气泡。

The Nabob

To the memory of William Hickey, Esq.

Coming out of India with ten thousand a year
Exchanged for flesh and temper, a dry Faust
Whose devil barters with digestion, has he paid dear
For dipping his fingers in the Roc's valley?

Who knows? It's certain that he owns a rage,
A face like shark-skin, full of Yellow Jack,
And that unreckoning tyranny of age
That calls for turtles' eggs in Twickenham.

Sometimes, by moonlight, in a barge he'll float
Whilst hirelings blow their skulking flageolets,
Served by a Rajah in a golden coat
With pigeon-pie... Madeira... and Madeira...

Or in his Bon de Paris with silver frogs
He rolls puff-bellied in an equipage,
Elegant chariot, through a gulf of fogs
To dine on dolphin-steak with Post-Captains.

Who knows? There are worse things than steak, perhaps,
Worse things than oyster-sauces and tureens
And worlds of provender like painted maps
Pricked out with ports of claret and pitchcocked eels,

And hubbubs of billiard-matches, burnt champagne,
Beautiful ladies "of the establishment"
Always in tempers, or melting out again,
Bailiffs and Burgundy and writs of judgment—

Thus to inhabit huge, lugubrious halls
Damp with the steam of entrees, glazed with smoke,
Raw drinking, greasy eating, bussing and brawls,
Drinking and eating and bursting into bed-chambers.

But, in the end, one says farewell to them;
And if he'd curse to-day—God damn your blood! —
Even his curses I'd not altogether condemn,
Not altogether scorn; and if phantoms ate—

Hickey, I'd say, sit down, pull up, set to:
Here's knife and fork, there's wine, and there's a barmaid.
Let us submerge ourselves in onion-soup,
Anything but this "damned profession of writing".

掠夺者

谨以此纪念威廉·希基先生

每年能用肉体和怒火从印度
换来一万镑，干瘪浮士德
用魔鬼来换消化，他是否已经为
染指洛克山谷而付出代价？

谁知道呢？他一定很生气，
脸似鲨鱼皮，染上黄热病，
未付出代价的暴政的时代
呼唤特威克纳姆的海龟蛋。

有时，月下，他乘驳船漂浮
雇工们吹着藏起的木笛，
身着金黄色外套的拉贾
奉上鸽肉派……白葡萄酒……和酒……

有时他会在巴黎与银色蛙

鼓着肚皮驾着装备齐全、
精致的马车，穿海湾浓雾
与邮局主管共享海豚肉。

谁知道呢？也许，还有不如，
海豚肉、牡蛎酱和陶罐的
还有成堆草料像地图上
葡萄酒与烤鳗的港口凸起。

台球赛的喧嚣，热烫的香槟，
"机构内"的姿容姣美的女士
脾气总是暴躁，也容易消气，
法警、勃艮第酒以及判决书——

住在巨大、阴凉的大厅里
被水蒸气润湿，被烟熏亮，
生饮酒、油腻饮食、喧闹争吵，
喝好酒吃好饭又立马冲进卧室。

但，最后，有人向他们告别；
若他今天诅咒你——该死的！——
即使是他的诅咒我也不会谴责，
不会蔑视；而如果幽灵吃下——

希基，我会说，坐，拉起，准备：

这里有刀叉、美酒和女招待。
让我们沉浸在洋葱汤中，
除了"该死的写作"，什么都行。

In A/C with Ghosts

You can shuffle and scuffle and scold,

    You can rattle the knockers and knobs,

Or batter the doorsteps with buckets of gold

    Till the Deputy-Governor sobs.

You can sneak up a suitable plank

    In a frantic endeavor to see—

But what do they do in the Commonwealth Bank

    When the Big Door bangs at Three?

Listen in the cellars, listen in the vaults,

Can't you hear the tellers turning somersaults?

Can't you hear the spectres of inspectors and directors

Dancing with the phantoms in a Dead Man's Waltz?

Some are ghosts of nabobs, poverty and stray bobs,

Midas and his mistress, Mammon and his wife;

Other ones are sentries, guarding double entries,

Long-forgotten, double-dealing, troubled double-life.

Down among the pass-books, money lent and spent,

Down among the forests of the Four Per Cent,

Where the ledgers meet and moulder, and the overdrafts grow older,

And the phantoms shrug a shoulder when you ask 'em for the rent.

They are bogies of Grandfather's cheques,

    They are spectres of buried accounts,

They are crinoline sweethearts with pearls on their necks,

    Demanding enormous amounts.

They are payment for suppers and flowers,

    For diamonds to banish a tear,

For sweet, pretty ladies in opulent hours...

    And tombstones... and bailiffs... and beer...

Down in the bowels of the bank, the ledgers lie rank upon rank,

The debts of the ages come out of their pages,

The bones of old loans creak and clank—

Oh, if you could peep through the door

To day at a Quarter Past Four,

You'd find all the ghosts at their usual posts,

And you wouldn't sign cheques any more!

在幽灵银行

你可以推诿扭打责骂，

    可以敲响门环和旋钮，

甚至可以用金桶猛砸门阶
　　直到副行长开始抽泣。
偷偷地靠近木板缝隙
　　带着一丝疯狂去窥视——
大门在三点钟响时他们在
　　联邦银行做什么？

你在地窖里听，在金库里听，
难道听不到柜员翻筋斗吗？
你听不见巡视员和经理们的恐惧
在与亡灵共舞死神华尔兹？
有些曾是无赖、穷人和流浪汉，
有富豪和情妇，富人和妻子；
还有哨兵，在守卫着双重门禁，
长久遗忘，双重交易，烦恼生活。
存折里，记录着借进和支出，
记载着百分之四利息之处，
账本已是破旧不堪，透支已是陈年旧账，
向亡灵索要租金，他们耸肩不予理睬。

它们是祖父支票之妖，
　　是被埋葬的账户之灵，
是挂着珍珠项链的衬裙甜心，
　　索要金额巨大之财。
它们支付晚餐还有鲜花，

购买钻石驱散泪珠，
在辉煌时期相伴的甜美女士……
　还有墓碑……管家……啤酒……

在银行的内部深处，账本层层叠叠堆放，
一页页账单陈述着积年欠款，
账本书脊嘎吱作响——
哦，若能透过门窥视
四点一刻你会发现，
亡灵们在银行各司其职，
你绝不会再签下支票！

Talbingo

"Talbingo River"—as one says of bones:
"Captain" or "Commodore" that smelt gunpowder
In old engagements no one quite believes
Or understands. Talbingo had its blood
As they did, ran with waters huge and clear
Lopping down mountains,
Turning crags to banks.

Now it's a sort of aching valley,
Basalt shaggy with scales,

A funnel of tobacco-coloured clay,
Smoulders of puffed earth
And pebbles and shell-bodied flies
And water thickening to stone in pocks.

That's what we're like out here,
Beds of dried-up passions.

塔宾戈

"塔宾戈河"——说到尸骨时说：
带着火药味的"船长"或"准将"
旧约定中无人完全相信
或者领悟。塔宾戈流淌的
是这样的血液，清澈洪流
顺山岭而下，
峭壁变堤岸。

如今它是个痛苦深渊，
岩石斑痕累累，
烟草色的淤泥堆积滞留，
地火在阴燃
鹅卵石还有甲壳虫
石上水洼蒸发留下污痕。

我们就是河床，
此刻激情干涸。

South Country

After the whey-faced anonymity
Of river-gums and scribbly-gums and bush,
After the rubbing and the hit of brush,
You come to the South Country

As if the argument of trees were done,
The doubts and quarrelling, the plots and pains,
All ended by these clear and gliding planes
Like an abrupt solution.

And over the flat earth of empty farms
The monstrous continent of air floats back
Coloured with rotting sunlight and the black,
Bruised flesh of thunderstorms.

Air arched, enormous, pounding the bony ridge,
Ditches and hutches, with a drench of light,
So huge, from such infinities of height,
You walk on the sky's beach

While even the dwindled hills are small and bare,
As if, rebellious, buried, pitiful,
Something below pushed up a knob of skull,
Feeling its way to air.

南之国

河水覆上莫名的乳清色
两岸林木一片枯萎凌乱，
枝干随着烈风倾轧击打，
此时你来到南国。

树木的争端似乎已停止，
猜疑与争吵，阴谋与沉痛，
这些巨大冲击突如其来
这一切全都终止。

平坦空旷的田野的上空
那骇人的巨大气流回转
染上炙人的阳光与黑暗，
和雷雨的侵袭。

大气流，蓄力，重击贫瘠山脊、
沟渠和棚屋，闪电的光影，

它硕大无朋，它高高在上，
似可漫步其上。

然而即使是在荒芜的山谷，
看着多么，叛逆，隐匿，卑微，
也被下方某物给予天梯，
体会向上之路。

新西兰

诗歌选译

Charlie Bowen (1830—1917)

查理·鲍恩诗一首

The Old Year and the New

We beheld the old year dying,
  In the country of our birth;
When the drifted snow was lying
  On the hard and frozen earth;

Where the love of home was round us,
  By the blazing Christmas fires;
And the love of country bound us
  To the hearth-stones of our sires.

But our sons will see the glory
  Of the young and springing year;
Where the green earth tells the story
  Of a younger hemisphere.

And the eve will lose its sadness
In the hopefulness of day, —
In a birth so full of gladness, —
In a death without decay.

But for us the morning's garland
Glistens still with evening's dew; —
We—the children of a far land,
And the fathers of a new.

For we still, though old affection,
Hear the old year's dying sigh,
Through the sad sweet recollection
Of the years that are gone by.

While, through all the future gleaming,
A bright golden promise runs,
And its happy light is streaming
On the greatness of our sons.

Pray we, then, whate'ver betide them—
Howsoever great they're grown—
That the past of England guide them,
While the present is their own!

辞旧迎新之时

我们目睹旧年逝去，
　　在我们出生之地；
雪花纷纷飘落盖住
　　坚硬冰冷的土地；

我们爱的家园就在，
　　熊熊的圣诞炉边；
我们对国家的热爱
　　缚于祖先的炉炭。

我们的孩子将看到
　　新年带来的荣光；
绿色地球将会介绍
　　春意盎然新气象。

在满怀憧憬的白日
　　黑夜也不再伤悲——
在欣欣然的新生里，
　　在未腐的死亡里。

我们看见清晨花饰
　　闪烁着昨夜露水——

我们——遥远国度之子，
　　也将新升为父辈。

旧情犹在，我们听见
　　旧年的临别叹息，
悲伤又甜蜜的思念
　　浸满逝去的日子。

然而，未来闪亮而来，
　　承诺光辉的前途，
幸福的光芒笼罩在
　　后代的伟大之处。

那么，祈祷吧，无论何事——
　　无论他们结果怎样——
以英格兰过往为史，
　　未来在他们手上！

Arnold Wall（1869—1966）
阿诺德·沃尔诗三首

The City from the Hills

There lies our city folded in the mist,
Like great meadow in an early morn
Flinging her spears of grass up through white films,
Each with its thousand thousand-tinted globes.

Above us such an air was poets' dream,
The clean and vast wing-winnowed clime of Heaven.

Each of her streets is closed with shining Alps,
Like Heaven at the end of long plain lives.

山上的城市

我们的城市在朦胧的雾中，

犹如清晨雾中的草坪
用它的草尖刺透了白雾,
顶着成千上万彩色水珠。

城市的空气是诗人之梦,
干净广阔微风吹拂的天堂。

光闪阿尔卑斯山的街道,
如漫长平凡一生的天堂。

The City in the Plains

In a silvern afternoon
We saw the city sleeping,
Sleeping and rustling a little
Under the brindled hills.
Spectres of Alps behind,
Alps behind and beyond,
Tall, naked, and blue.
The city sleeps in the plain—
A flight of glittering scales
Flung in a wanton curve,
Sinking softly to earth
Flung from a Titan's palm.

In the silver afternoon
All round the shining city,
A thousand thousand sheaves
Loll in the golden plain;
On goes the stately wain,
The dun hind striding by it,
Beside the elms and willows,
Between the Alps and the sea.

平原上的城市

在一个银色午后
看见沉睡的城市
在那斑驳的山脚下
沙沙声微响。
阿尔卑斯前后，
天空连绵不绝，
高，无云，碧蓝。
城市沉睡在平原——
是太阳神抛出的
明亮闪烁的鳞片
抛出随意曲线，
轻落在那平原。
在一个银色午后
成千上万束银光

歇在金色平原，
布满整座城市；
华贵马车不断，
褐色马蹄在行进，
在榆树和柳树边
阿尔卑斯和海间。

The Spell Broken

The music ceases;
Glory slips from the pines
And is tripped from the high hill;
The world, that stood still,
Resumes her hobbling gait
And will catch her train yet.

打破魔咒

音乐声已停；
光落于松枝间
绊倒在高山之巅；
世界，停下来，
又复蹒跚步态
追赶时光列车。

Mary Ursula Bethell（1874—1945）
玛丽·厄休拉·贝瑟尔诗六首

Response

When you wrote your letter it was April,
And you were glad that it was spring weather,
And that the sun shone out in turn with showers of rain.

I write in waning May and it is autumn,
And I am glad that my chrysanthemums
Are tied up fast to strong posts,
So that the south winds cannot beat them down.
I am glad that they are tawny coloured,
And fiery in the low west evening light.
And I am glad that one bush warbler
Still sings in the honey-scented wattle...

But oh, we have remembering hearts,

And we say "How green it was in such and such an April,"
And "Such and such an autumn was very golden,"
And "Everything is for a very short time."

回信

你写信的时候还是四月，
你很庆幸当时恰是春季，
时而天空放晴时而阵雨又淋漓。

我回信已是五月末的秋季，
我庆幸自己早早将菊花
绑在牢固木杆上，
这样就不会被南风吹垮。
我欣喜于这茶色的菊花
被西面低处的夜灯照亮。
我欣喜看到一只黄莺
在蜂蜜香的篱笆上啼啭……

但是，我们的心会回忆，
我们会说"那时那刻四月绿得肆意"，
"那时那刻的秋季满目金黄色"，
"美好的事物总是转瞬即逝"。

Erica

Sit down with me awhile beside the heath-corner.

Here have I laboured hour on hour in winter,
Digging thick clay, breaking up clods, and draining,
Carrying away cold mud, bringing up sandy loam,
Bringing these rocks and setting them all in their places,
To be shelter from winds, shade from too burning sun.

See, now, how sweetly all these plants are springing
Green, ever green, and flowering turn by turn,
Delicate heaths, and their fragrant Australian kinsmen,
Shedding, as once unknown in New Holland, strange scents on
    the air,
And purple and white daboecia—the Irish heather—
Said in the nurseryman's list to be so well suited
For small gardens, for rock gardens, and for graveyards.

石楠花

同我在石南花边的角落坐坐。

冬天我每时每刻在此辛苦劳作，

挖厚黏土，捣碎土块，又排水，
挖走冰冷的泥土，然后铺上沃土，
把石块都搬到它们应放的地方，
免受狂风侵袭，避免烈日暴晒。

看，现在，这些植物长得多好
绿色，常青，花团一簇接一簇，
娇嫩石楠和芬芳澳大利亚同属，
散发着，曾不为新荷兰人所知的气味，
紫色和白色的——爱尔兰石楠花——
是苗圃老板罗列的品类中最适合
小花园、岩石花园和墓地的花。

Dirge

Easter. And leaves falling.

Easter. And first autumn rains.

Easter. And dusk stealing

Our bright working daylight;

And cold night coming down

In which we may not work.

Easter. And morning bells

Chime in the late dark.

Soon those fluttering birds
Will seek a more genial clime.
Time has come to light fires
For lack of enlivening sun.

Summer's arrow is spent,
Stored her last tribute.
So, now, we plant our bulbs
With assured vision,
And, now, we sow our seeds
Sagely for sure quickening.

So, purging our borders
We burn all rubbish up,
That all weak and waste growth,
That all unprofitable weeds,
All canker and corrosion,
May be consumed utterly.

These universal bonfires
Have a savour of sacrifice.
See how their clean smoke,
Ruddy and white whorls,
Rises to the still heavens
In plumy spirals.

You take me—yes, I know it—
Fresh from your vernal Lent.
These ashes I will now spread
For nutriment about the roses,
Dust unto fertile dust,
And say no word more.

悼

复活节。叶凋零。
复活节。秋雨初至。
复活节。暮色降
偷走明亮日光；
寒夜终于来临
我们停止劳作。

复活节。晨钟在
黎明前敲响。
那些飞鸟即将
奔向温暖的南方。
时间已是熹微
此刻应当点亮篝火。

夏日时光已逝，
留秋的礼赞。

因此，现在，出于
远见种球茎，
然后，现在，聪明
地为复苏播下种子。

所以，清理边缘，
烧毁所有垃圾，
所有脆弱植物，
所有的无益的杂草，
所有溃烂的腐物，
可能会全部清除。

随处可见的篝火
散发出牺牲的气味。
看洁净烟雾，
红白色烟火，
如羽毛般盘旋至
寂静的天宇。

在春光中——对，我知——
你来带走了我。
我将这灰烬播撒
变成玫瑰花丛的营养，
化为肥沃土壤，
默默无言语。

Decoration

This jar of roses and carnations on the window-sill,
Crimson upon sky-grey and snow-wrapt mountain-pallor,
(Sharp storm's asseveration of cold winter's on-coming,)
How strange their look, how lovely, rich and foreign,
The living symbol of a season put away.

A letter-sheaf, bound up by time-frayed filament,
I found; laid by; youth's flowering.
The exotic words blazed up blood-red against death's shadow,
Red upon grey. Red upon grey.

装饰花束

窗台上这一瓶红色玫瑰和康乃馨，
映在灰色天空和远山的积雪上，
（暴风雨预示着寒冷冬日即将来临，）
它们真奇怪，可爱，华丽，新奇，
花瓶留下了一个过往的季节。

我找到，一捆信件，绑线被岁月，
摧残；搁置；青春繁花。

陌生话语在死亡灰里迸发出血红，

红映着灰，红映着灰。

Lever de Rideau

Today

the clocks strike

seven, seven, seven, and church-bells

chime busily, and the plain-town heavily wakes;

a salt-sharp east wind flicks and swells

and tosses my emerald silk curtains;

translucent green on blue the empyrean, and lo!

north and west, endlessly limned and painted,

my mountains, my mountains, all snow.

Now a change begins in the heavenly tone-chord;

to the east, eyes! where the sea is incised

like azure ice on sky of vermeil;

oh, dream on prolonged, beautiful prelude!

hushed still, delay, summoning bird-song!

hold, magic touch, be arrested, lovely crisis of sunrise!

when yonder death-white summits are rose-flushed

and glittering, I must

away.

把帷幕拉开

今天
钟声鸣
七点，七点，七点，教堂的
钟声长鸣，平原小镇沉沉苏醒；
刺骨的东风席卷着
掀动我翡翠绿丝质帷幔；
快看，那翠绿映衬着蓝色苍穹！
从北到西，无尽地描绘着，
我的山，我的山，雪山。

天籁般的和弦现已发生变化；
眼，看东方！大海像天蓝的
冰镶嵌着朱红色晨曦；
哦，悠长的梦在，美丽的前奏！
沉静，绵长，召唤鸟鸣声！
抓住，像魔术手法般，逮住，喜人的日出！
当白色远山泛着玫瑰红
闪闪发光，我必
离去。

October Morning

"All clear, all clear, all clear!" after the storm in the morning
The birds sing; all clear the rain-scoured firmament,
All clear the still blue horizontal sea;
And what, all white again? All white the long line of the mountains
And clear on sky's sheer blue intensity.

Gale raved night-long, but all clear, now, in the sunlight
And sharp, earth-scented air, a fair new day.
The jade and emerald squares of far-spread cultivated
All clear, and powdered foot-hills, snow-fed waterway,
And every black pattern of plantation made near;
All clear, the city set—but oh for taught interpreter,
To translate the quality, the excellence, for initiate seer
To tell the essence of this hallowed clarity,
Reveal the secret meaning of the symbol: "clear".

十月的早晨

"清澈，清澈，清澈！"早上的暴风雨过后
鸟在唱；雨后天空如此清澈，
清澈平静的蓝色海平面；
然后，又变白？连绵的群山的白色轮廓

在天的深蓝中变得清澈。

整夜狂风肆虐，现在，阳光明媚
清新，泥土香气，全新一天。
满目皆是玉石和翡翠的通透光泽
清净，山麓飘雪，水沟积雪覆盖，
白雪之下是春播的黑色土地；
清净，城市仿佛是——经验丰富的译者，
要把这眼前的清净，完美转译，而预言家
将要讲述这清净空灵的本质，
他要揭示这"清"字的神秘含义。

John Russell Hervey（1889—1958）
约翰・罗素・赫维诗二首

Threnos

Each day sees die the lonely leaf, sees die
The perfect paw, the unobstructed wing,
    Sees stooping from the arena
    The flesh with death on shoulder.

These are the fringes of disaster announcing
The slow, mesmeric tide, the heedless wash,
    And here my proud ones gather
    The bone, the claw, the feather.

But where the moon of wonder lights the forest,
And love looks out of the window, and the white wing
    Of song relents no augur
    Hints of the destroyer.

Or so I considered until the emissary,

And now each day sees die the dream, the lover:

    Ah, who will stand for ever,

    Out of this coil deliver?

哀颂

每天看见孤叶凋零，动物
死去，鸟儿不再振翅飞行，
    斗兽场上鲜血淋漓
    肩膀预告了死讯。

这是在宣告蛊惑人心的灾难
如无情的潮水，慢慢，蔓延，
    自以为是的人们
    还在收骨、爪、羽毛。

神奇月光照亮森林的地方，
仁爱望向窗外，而歌声的
    白翅没有预示出
    毁灭者的行迹。

我一直如此思考直至天使看到，
现在，梦和仁爱每天在消逝：

啊，谁能永远摆脱，
持续不断地纷杂？

Two Old Men Look at the Sea

They do not speak but into their empty mood
　　Receive the leaden utterance of waves,
　　And intimations blowing from old graves,
　　Men who have already crossed to the torpid sandspit
　　Between life and death, whose cold rejected hands
　　Have flung farewell to passion, the brassy lands
　　Of love and pursuit, who even taste not life
　　In the pomp of passing synopsis, but only savour
　　The salty wind and sand swirling up to claim
　　The total mystery masking in a name.

How shall we live and hold, how love and handle
　　To the last beach the dark and difficult gleanings?
　　For so must we come, hugging our recompense,
　　To the unfeeling shore, to the bleak admonitory tide,
　　Our fear being as a hand that cups a candle
　　Against the winds that whiff away pretence,
　　And the sea whose sentence strikes like a leaden wave.

两位老者在看海

他们没有言语，他们平静地
　　接收着海浪低沉的声音，
　　听到古墓里传出的话语，
　　说着那些人已穿过生死之间的
　　沙洲，他们用冰冷僵硬的手
　　挥别激情和象征着热爱与
　　追求的黄土地；再品尝不到
　　在浮华中逝去的生机，却只能品味
　　咸的风和盘旋而来的沙尘
　　诉说隐藏在名字里的神秘。

如何珍视生活，喜爱并收拾
　　最后海滩上黑色难捡的物品？
　　因此必须来这，无情的海岸，
　　和阴冷的潮水，我们怀抱大海的补偿，
　　恐惧却好像是捧着蜡烛的手
　　抵挡着汹涌袭来的海风，
　　以及吐着铅灰色波浪的大海。

Darcy Cresswell（1896—1960）
达西·克雷斯韦尔诗二首

O England

O England, why do you hasten to fall and forget your spring,

Like the leaves that hurry down from the trees in the autumn,

To whirl away over the earth with the following wind,

To lead the way for the year's load of snow,

Which is Death that follows for ever the marching summer of life,

Having now only the weak sun of remember'd song,

Only cities that shrouds, only poets that are tombs?

英格兰

啊英格兰，你为何遗忘春天急于入秋，

就像秋天枝头的树叶匆匆地飘落，

在大地上与跟随而至的狂风共舞，

为一年将至的大雪引路，

它就是夏日的生机逝去后遗下的残骸，
仅留回忆中歌曲里的微弱阳光，
仅有城市是裹尸布，诗人是坟墓？

Summer's Sadness

Ripe trees, could you but hear
The cold winds coming near;
Poor boughs, could you but see
The curl'd leaves as they flee;
Did memory but keep
It's green to grieve your sleep;
Oh then, you trees and flowers,
Your summer were as ours!

夏日悲歌

树，你是否听清
冷风脚步渐近；
可怜枝丫，是否
看见枯叶逃走；
绿仅存于回忆
悲切在你梦里；
如此，树木和芳菲，
与我夏日无异！

Arthur Rex Duggard Fairburn（1904—1957）
阿瑟·雷克斯·杜加德·费尔伯恩诗五首

Winter Night

The candles gutter and burn out,
　　and warm and snug we take our ease,
and faintly comes the wind's great shout
　　as he assails the frozen trees.

The vague walls of this little room
　　contract and close upon the soul;
deep silence hangs amid the gloom;
　　no sound but the small voice of the coal.

Here in this sheltered firelit place
　　we know not wind nor shivering tree;
we two alone inhabit space,
　　locked in our small infinity.

This is our world, where love enfolds
　　all images of joy, all strife
resolves in peace: this moment holds
　　within its span the sum of life.

For Time's a ghost: these reddening coals
　　were forest once ere he'd begun,
and now from dark and timeless boles
　　we take the harvest of the sun;

and still the flower-lit solitudes
　　are radiant with the springs he stole
where violets in those buried woods
　　wake little blue flames in the coal.

Great stars may shine above this thatch;
　　beyond these walls perchance are men
with laws and dreams: but our thin latch
　　holds all such things beyond our ken.

The fire that lights our cloudy walls
　　now fails beneath the singing pot,
and as the last flame leaps and falls
　　the far wall is and then is not.

Now lovelier than firelight is the gleam
　　of dying embers, and your face
shines through the pathways of my dream
　　like young leaves in a forest place.

冷冬夜

烛光摇曳终于熄灭，
　　我们在温暖安逸中，
依稀听见狂风拍击
　　冻结的树干的吼声。

小屋的粗糙的墙壁
　　灵魂亦甘心于捆绑；
幽暗房内无声无息；
　　只有木炭燃烧的声响。

炭火点亮了小屋
　　忘记了风和战栗的树；
天地间仅余下你我，
　　安居于小小的一隅。

我们在这爱的世界，
　　烦忧消于宁静、欢乐

尽皆在此，一生时光
　似乎都浓缩在此刻。

时间像幽灵：烧红的炭
　很久以前曾是林木，
从历经岁月的黑炭
　现在我们收获暖阳；

鲜花点燃的孤炭仍然
　因它偷去春光火红
下面木头紫光闪闪
　点燃煤炭蓝色火焰。

茅屋之上群星闪烁；
　人们则在屋墙之外
有梦有法：但是这些
　全被细闩挡在屋外。

炉上陶罐尽情欢唱
　模糊屋墙火光渐暗，
一缕青烟跳起熄灭
　对面墙壁逐渐暗淡。

此时比火光更加喜人
　是余烬成灰的微光

照亮我梦中的小径
　　就像嫩叶之于森林。

Tapu

To stave off disaster, or bring the devil to heel,
　　or to fight against fear, some carry a ring or a locket,
but I, who have nothing to lose by the turn of the wheel,
　　and nothing to gain, I carry the world in my pocket.

For all I have gained, and have lost, is locked up in this thing,
　　this cup of cracked bone from the skull of a fellow long dead,
with a hank of thin yellowish hair fastened in with a ring.
　　For a symbol of death and desire these tokens are wed.

The one I picked out of a cave in a windy cliff-face
　　where the old Maoris slept, with a curse on the stranger who moved,
in despite of tapu, but a splinter of bone from that place.
　　The other I cut from the head of the woman I loved.

禁忌

为了躲避灾难，或者让恶魔屈服，
　　或为战胜恐惧，有人戴着项链或戒指，

生命车轮滚滚而过，而我这样的人，
　　无谓得失，我所拥有的尽在口袋里。

因为我的所有，全都锁在这东西里，
　　那是一个早已死去的人的碎头骨，
用环状物固定的一束淡黄色的头发。
　　这些交缠的物品象征死亡与欲望。

我在有风的悬崖边山洞里捡到它
　　毛利人就沉睡在那里。打破禁忌带走
那块头骨的人，将会受到他们的诅咒。
　　而另一块砍自我爱的女人的头骨。

A Farewell

What is there left to be said?
There is nothing we can say,
nothing at all to be done
to undo the time of day;
no words to make the sun roll east,
or raise the dead.

I loved you as I love life:
the hand I stretched out to you

returning like Noah's dove

brought a new earth to view,

till I was quick with love;

but Time sharpens his knife.

Time smiles and whets his knife,

and something has got to come out

quickly, and be buried deep,

not spoken or thought about

or remembered even in sleep.

You must live, get on with your life.

再不见

还有什么可说呢？

其实已无话可说，

也已经无事可做

打发这多余时刻；

话语不能驱使太阳

东升，唤醒死寂。

我曾爱你如生命：

向你伸出的手像

挪亚之鸽带去

陆地喜讯返航，

直至爱意消逝；
时间磨尖刀刃。

笑着把刀刺出，
有些事物必然快速
砍去，再深埋心底，
不再说起或思虑
睡梦中都不再回忆。
你只能，将生活继续。

The Encounter

As I set out on my journey
the sun was pale in the east,
and out of the frosty silence
ambled a strange beast.

The sun was shining bleakly,
the frost was thick and white,
it seemed the world had ended,
so calm it was, and bright.

I saw that the beast was youthful
and had lived since time began;

his head was horned and handsome,
he spoke with the tongue of a man.

"Turn back, for the way is endless,
the journey is in vain."
I looked at his eyes and saw there
my own in the glass of pain.

No vapour clouded his nostrils,
there were no tracks in the frost.
I looked in the eyes of the creature
and knew that we both were lost.

偶然相遇

我踏上旅程的时候
东方才刚刚露白，
在冷寂中一头怪兽
缓缓地走来。

此时日光仍熹微，
地上布满白霜，
如此的寂静、光亮，
好似世界已亡。

那怪兽看上去青壮
它仿佛来自远古；
长着角，面容俊俏，
张口说话发出男声。

"回头吧，前路无尽头，
这旅行必徒劳。"
望进他的眼我看见
我眼中满是痛楚。

它的鼻孔没有雾气，
霜冻中没有痕迹。
我凝视着怪兽的眼睛
我俩已迷失方位。

I'm Older than You, Please Listen

To the young man, I would say:
Get out! Look sharp, my boy,
before the roots are down,
before the equations are struck,
before a face or a landscape
has power to shape or destroy.
This land is a lump without leaven,

a body that has no nerves.
Don't be content to live in
a sort of second-grade heaven
with first-grade butter, fresh air,
and paper in every toilet;
becoming a butt for the malice
of those who have stayed and soured,
staying in turn to sour,
to smile, and savage the young.
If you're enterprising and able,
smuggle your talents away,
hawk them in livelier markets
where people are willing to pay.
If you have no stomach for roughage,
if patience isn't your religion,
if you must have sherry with your bitters,
if money and fame are your pigeon,
if you feel that you need success
and long for a good address,
don't anchor here in the desert—
the fishing isn't so good:
take a ticket for Megalopolis,
don't' stay in this neighborhood!

请你听听，老者之言

年轻人，请听我说：
去闯吧！赶紧，孩子，
趁着还未扎根，
趁着一切还未定形，
趁着面容还未沧桑
趁着人生前景未明。
此地是未发酵的面团，
缺乏勇气的躯干。
切勿满足于眼前
那一流的黄油、空气、
提供纸巾的厕所；
这里并非完美天堂；
人们说着酸话而你是
他们恶意的枪靶，
你会渐渐同化，
笑着，羞辱新一代。
如果有进取心和能力，
你就该出去闯荡，
到活跃市场兜售
自然会有人买下。
如果你并不甘于平淡，
如果闲散非你的信条，

如果你盼望着生活奢华，
如果金钱名誉是所求，
如果你梦想着成功
能入住高级住所，
那就别在沙漠抛锚——
此处的收成不好：
买张去大都市的车票吧，
不要在这里逗留！

Robin Hyde（1906—1936）
罗宾·海德诗一首

The Deserted Village

In the deserted village, sunken down
With a shrug of last weak old age, pulled back to earth,
All people are fled or killed. The cotton crop rots,
Not one mild house leans sideways, a man on crutches,
Not a sparrow earns from the naked floors,
Walls look, but cannot live without the folk they loved—
It would be a bad thing to awaken them.
Having broken the rice-bowl, seek not to fill it again.

The village temple, well built, with five smashed gods, ten whole
　　ones,
Does not want prayers. Its last vain prayer bled up
When the woman ran outside to be slain.
A temple must house its sparrows or fall asleep,

Therefore a long time, under his crown of snails,

The gilded Buddha demands to mediate,

No little flowering fires on the incense-strings

Startle Kwan-Yin, whom they dressed in satin—

Old women sewing beads like pearls in her hair.

This was a temple for the very poor ones:

Their gods were mud and lath: but artfully

Some village painter coloured them all.

Wooden dragons were carefully carved.

Finding in mangled wood one smiling childish tree,

Roses and bells not one foot high,

I set it back, at the feet of Kwan-Yin.

A woman's prayer-bag,

Having within her paper prayers, paid for in copper,

Seeing it torn, I gathered it up.

I shall often think, "The woman I did not see

Voiced here her dying wish.

But the gods dreamed on. So low her voice, so loud

The guns, all that death-night, who would stop to hear?"

荒废了的村庄

在这荒芜的村庄，伴随着

最后一间老屋倒下，归于尘土，

村民或逃或死，棉花烂地里，

路边不见房屋，或拄拐杖的人，
裸露的地面引不来麻雀，
墙在看，离开他们爱的人难活——
唤醒它们可不是件好事情。
已经打破的饭碗，别再把它盛满饭。

精美村庙，五座神像粉碎，余十座，
不再有香客。最后一位血流尽
女香客逃出寺庙仍被屠。
庙只有留住麻雀才不死寂，
头戴蜗牛冠，菩萨金光闪闪，
需要很长时间来沉思默想。
观音不为香柱上小火苗所动
人们给她穿上绫罗绸缎——
老妇缝珍珠念珠进她发中。
这个才是穷人供奉的寺庙：
佛身由泥土和板条制成，
乡村画师巧妙地上色。
木龙的制作精雕细琢。
残林中一株小树孩童般微笑，
玫瑰铃铛放得很低，
我把它放回到，观音脚边。
妇人的香袋里，
装着她的祈祷纸文，她用铜钱买来，
见它撕破，我把它捡起。

我常想起，"我没见这妇人在此

说出心中遗愿。

神还在做梦。妇人声低，枪声

大作。死亡之夜，谁屈尊聆听？"

Charles Brasch（1909—1973）
查尔斯·布拉什诗五首

The Islands

Always, in these islands, meeting and parting
Shake us, making tremulous the salt-rimmed air;
Divided and perplexed the sea is waiting,
Birds and fishes visit us and disappear.

The future and the past stand at our doors,
Beggars who for one look of trust will open
Worlds that can answer our unknown desires,
Entering us like rain and sun to ripen.

Remindingly beside the quays, the white
Ships lie smoking; and from their haunted bay
The godwits vanished towards another summer.
Everywhere in light and calm the murmuring

Shadow of departure; distance looks our way;

And none knows where he will lie down at night.

这些岛

这些岛屿，总是，相遇又分离

震动了我们，和咸味的空气；

海水破碎后又合一等待着，

那些海鸟与鱼的来来去去。

未来与过去在门口站立，

在对信任的乞求中开启了

我们对未知欲望的世界，

如骄阳如暴雨迎接着我们。

在码头边醒目的是，白船

停泊着冒着烟；塍鹬远离

栖息的海湾，消失在下个夏季。

风和日丽中处处可闻离别

呢喃的阴霾；前路如此漫漫；

不知夜晚它将停歇何地。

Envoy's Report

I found him sitting in his upper room and his back leant against a window and the waves of the great Syrian Sea beat their spray against his neck.

—*Journey of Wen-Amen*

Behind his head the waves played;
His face was towards the hollow room.
Full in the tide of light I stood
And could not see his lips move
Nor the quick brows; and his voice came
Folded in the roll of waves
That echoed through the room, and ceased,
But nothing eased the beating sea,
And ignorant what he had said
I waited. And again he spoke
And louder, and across the sky
A drift of cloud muffled the stroke
Of water, and his voice rang clear
From still head and invisible mouth,
Each word took shape upon the light
And entered into eye and ear.
I bowed. The shadow left the sea;

As the waves fell. And bowing once yet
Before the unmoving king, eyes dropped
I passed through shade and shade and out.

特使公告

　　我看见他坐正在他楼上的那个房间，背靠着窗户，叙利亚海的浪花在拍打着他的脖子。

——温·阿蒙的旅途

海浪在身后嬉戏；
他面对着空旷的房间。
而我背对着光站着
看不清他的口型
或他的表情；海浪声
在房间里回荡着
盖住说话声，他暂停，
但海浪仍不停拍打，
不明白他所说的话
我只能等待。他只好
提高音量，团云忽然
遮盖了击打的海浪，
面容和口型，仍模糊
说话的声音却已清晰，
言语在日光中成形

终于可见也可听见。
我鞠躬听令。云飘去；
海浪消停。发号施令的
大使面前，我低垂着眼
在暗影中躬身退去。

Forerunners

Not by us was the unrecorded stillness
Broken, and in their monumental dawn
The rocks, the leaves unveiled;
Those who were before us trod first the soil.

And named the bays and mountains; while round them spread
The indefinable currents of the human,
That still about their chosen places
Trouble the poignant air.

But their touch was light; warm in their hearts holding
The land's image, they had no need to impress themselves
Like conquerors, scarring it with vain memorials.
They had no fear of being forgotten.

In the face of our different coming they retreated,

But without panic, not disturbing the imprint

Of their living upon the air, which continued

To speak of them to the rocks and sombre, guarded lakes.

The earth holds them

As the mountains hold the shadows by day

In their powerful repose, only betrayed by a lingering

Twilight in the hooded ravines.

Behind our quickness, our shallow occupation of the easier

Landscape, their unprotecting memory

Mildly hovers, surrounding us with perspective,

Offering soil for our rootless behaviour.

先行者

并不是我们打破这里未知

的宁静，在丰碑式的黎明

岩石、树叶显露；

吾之先辈踏上这片土地。

为海湾山脉命名；由此散开

一代接着一代在此繁衍生息，

在他们所选择的地方

烦扰伤感空气。

但是他们触摸轻柔；对这片
土地心怀温情，他们不需留下征服
的印记，虚假的纪念成为伤痕。
他们没有被遗忘的恐惧。

面对我们代代的降临，他们退去，
平静地，不打扰他们赖以生存
的空气，继续讲述他们的故事
给岩石，给被守护着的幽暗湖泊。

大地守护
它们如深沉休眠的高山
守护日落晚影，黑暗笼罩的山谷只留下
那一线逗留的暮光。

我们迅速地、轻易地享用着这块土地的
风景，其不受保护的记忆
缓缓地盘旋，留下了真知灼见，
为我们无根行为提供土壤。

The Silent Land

The mountains are empty. No hermits have hallowed the caves,

Nor has the unicorn drunk from the green fountain
Whose poplar shadow never heard the horn.
Lives like a vanishing night-dew drop away.

The sea casts up its wreckage, ship or shell,
Beams of day and darkness guardedly
Break on the savage forests that from groins
And armpits of the hills so fiercely look.

The plains are nameless and the cities cry for meaning,
The unproved heart still seeks a vein of speech
Beside the sprawling rivers, in the stunted township,
By the pine windbreak where the hot wind bleeds.

Man must lie with the gaunt hills like a lover,
Earning their intimacy in the calm sigh
Of a century of quiet and assiduity,
Discovering what solitude has meant.

Before our headlong time broke on these waters,
And in himself unite time's dual order;
For he to both the swift and slow belongs,
Formed for a hard and complex history.

So relenting, earth will tame her tamer,

And speak with all her voices tenderly

To seal his homecoming to world. Ah then

For him the Oreads will haunt the fields near the snowline,

He will walk with his shadow across the bleaching plain

No longer solitary, and hear the sea talking

Dark in the rocks, O and the angel will visit,

Signing life's air with indefinable mark.

沉默土地

空山。没有隐士来将洞穴奉为神圣，

也没有独角兽来此喝过映着

白杨树倒影的碧绿泉水。

生命就像是一滴夜露消逝。

海浪抛起贝壳、船的残骸，

日光和暗影界限分明

守护自山谷到山顶都是

肆意生长着的原始森林。

平原无名而城市在呼唤着意义，

在延绵的河畔，在未发展

的小镇，未经证实的心仍然还在

寻找着它那话语的脉络。

人类需与嶙峋的山峦同在，
在百年寂静和辛勤发出的
叹息中与山川犹如恋人般的亲密，
探寻着孤独的真实含义。

我们的时间仓促闯入水中，
以其本身重整二者的顺序；
它既缓慢地而又飞速地，
形成艰难且复杂的历史。

大地，将驯服她的开垦者，
说着她所有的温柔话语
封印时间逆流的途径。啊
它见精灵在雪线边的田野出没，

它带着它的身影穿过皑皑平原
不再感到孤独，还能听见大海
在谈论着岩石，哦天使将来临，
为空气烙上不知名的印记。

Great Sea

Kona Coast, Hawaii

Speak for us, great sea.

Speak in the night, compelling
The frozen heart to hear,
The memoried to forget.
O speak, until your voice
Possesses the night and bless
The separate and fearful;
Under folded darkness
All the lost unite—
Each to each discovered,
Vowed and wrought by your voice
And in your life, that holds
And penetrates our life:
You from whom we rose,
In whom our power lives on.

All night, all night till dawn
Speak for us, great sea.

大海

科纳海（岸），夏威夷

大海，说话呀。

在夜里说，让那些
冰冷的心听见，
将不堪回忆忘却。
说吧，直到声音
掌控黑夜赐福
孤独以及恐惧；
让迷失的人在
黑暗中团结——
发现人人向你
宣誓为你音动
你的一生，影响
渗透我们生命：
你是驱动力，
力量因你而延续。

整夜，直到天明
大海，说话呀。

加拿大

诗歌选译

Charles Heavysege（1816—1876）
查尔斯·海维塞奇诗一首

Sonnet—Winter Night

The stars are setting in the frosty sky,
　　Numerous as pebbles on a broad sea coast;
While o'er the vault the cloud-like galaxy
　　Has marshalled its innumerable host.
Alive all heaven seems: with wondrous glow,
　　Tenfold refulgent every star appears;
As if some wide, celestial gale did blow,
　　And thrice illume the ever-kindled spheres.
Orbs, with glad orbs rejoicing, burning, beam
　　Ray-crowned, with lambent lustre in their zones;
Till o'er the blue, bespangled spaces seem
　　Angels and great archangels on their thrones; —

A host divine, whose eyes are sparkling gems,
　　And forms more bright than diamond diaderms.

十四行（诗）——冬夜

霜冻的天空里落下星星，
　　繁如辽阔海岸上的鹅卵石；
在穹顶之上，云朵般的银河
　　呈现出了无数不同样貌。
天宇似有生命：光亮无比，
　　每颗星星闪着十倍光辉；
仿佛一阵狂风吹过天际，
　　多次照亮永不灭的球体。
光球，带着欢欣，燃烧，亮闪
　　戴着光冠，淡黄色的光泽；
直照射在蓝色、发光的空间
　　天使和大天使坐在宝座——
神圣主人，眼是发光宝钻，
　　光亮胜过那钻石的王冠。

Alexander McLachlan（1818—1896）
亚历山大·麦克拉克伦诗一首

Garibaldi

O sons of Italy awake,
Your hearths and altars are at stake,
—Arise, arise, for Freedom's sake,
　　And strike with Garibaldi!

The Liberator now appears,
Foretold by prophets, bards and seers,
The hero sprung from blood and tears,
　　All hail to Garibaldi!

Let serfs and cowards fear and quake, —
O Venice, Naples, Rome awake,
Like lava of your burning lake,
　　Rush on with Garibaldi!

Up and avenge your country's shame,
Like Athena belching forth her flame,
Rush on in freedom's holy name,
　　And strike with Garibaldi!

'Tis freedom thunders in your ears;
The weary night of blood and tears,
The sorrows of a thousand years,
　　Cry, on with Garibaldi!

The shades that hover round your fanes,
The blood of heroes in your veins,
Keep shouting, rise and break your chains,
　　And on with Garibaldi!

And tongues in many a dungeon stone,
And prison walls are shouting on,
And sweep the madman from his throne,
　　Then on with Garibaldi!

The Roman Eagle is not dead,
Her mighty wings again are spread,
To swoop upon the tyrant's head,
　　And strike with Garibaldi!

The drum of Bomba's doom does beat,

The shadows of the murdered meet,

To drag him to the judgment seat,

    Then on with Garibaldi!

The land wherein the laurel waves,

Was never meant to nourish slaves,

Then onward to your bloody graves,

    Or live like Garibaldi!

加里波第

哦意大利之子已醒，

你火炉和祭坛已危，

——起来，起来，为了自由，

    和加里波第共战！

预言解放者已出现，

先知、诗人和预言家，

英雄从血泪中诞生，

    向加里波第致敬！

让附庸和懦夫惊恐——

哦，威尼斯、那不勒斯、

罗马，如湖中的熔岩，
　和加里波第前进！

为国家的耻辱复仇，
像雅典娜喷出火焰，
以自由的圣名前进，
　和加里波第共战！

自由在你耳边轰鸣；
血与泪的疲惫之夜，
一千年不去的悲伤，
　哭吧，与加里波第！

那神庙四周的阴影，
血管里英雄的鲜血，
怒吼，起来，挣断枷锁，
　与加里波第共进！

地牢里面无数的人舌，
监狱的墙壁在呼喊，
把疯子从王座赶下，
　与加里波第共进！

罗马之鹰并未死去，
再次怒张有力翅膀，

猛然扑向暴君头颅，
　　和加里波第共战！

邦巴末日之鼓敲响，
被杀者的魂灵到来，
把他拖到审判席上，
　　与加里波第共战！

月桂枝舞动的土地，
绝对不会豢养奴隶，
要么走向血腥墓地，
　　或生如加里波第！

Charles Sangster（1822—1893）
查尔斯·桑斯特诗八首

The Thousand Islands

Here the Spirit of beauty keepeth
    Jubilee for evermore;
Here the voice of gladness leapeth,
    Echoing from shore to shore.
O'er the hidden watery valley,
    O'er each buried wood and glade,
Dances our delighted galley,
    Through the sunlight and the shade—
Dances o'er the granite cells,
    Where the soul of beauty dwells:

Here the flowers are ever springing,
    While the summer breezes blow;
Here the Hours are ever clinging,

Loitering before they go;
Playing around each beauteous islet,
　　Loath to leave the sunny shore,
Where, upon her couch of violet,
　　Beauty sits for evermore—
Sits and smiles by day and night,
　　Hand in hand with pure Delight.

Here the Spirit of beauty dwelleth
　　In each palpitating tree,
In each amber wave that welleth
　　From its home beneath the sea;
In the moss upon the granite,
　　In each calm, secluded bay,
With the zephyr trains that fan it
　　With their sweet breaths all the day—
On the waters, on the shores,
　　Beauty dwelleth evermore!

一千座岛屿

美丽之神永远在此
　　带来欢乐的庆典；
快乐的笑声起伏，
　　在海岸之间呼应。

在隐蔽的水下山谷之上，
　　在树林和空地之上，
大帆船愉快地掠过，
　　穿过光影的交织——
在花岗岩块上掠过，
　　美丽的灵魂栖息：

这里的鲜花永不凋零，
　　夏日的暖风吹拂；
这里时间放缓脚步，
　　徘徊着不肯离去；
在美丽的小岛上玩耍，
　　阳光海岸不愿离，
这里，紫罗兰花榻上，
　　美丽在此永停息——
日夜停留笑眯眯，
　　与单纯喜悦一起。

美丽之神永远在此
　　在每棵颤动之树，
从海底翻涌而上
　　琥珀色的浪花上；
在花岗岩的苔藓上，
　　宁静，隐蔽海湾上，
和风整日不停吹拂

带来香甜的气息——
在水上，在海岸上，
　美丽永远栖息！

The Rapid

All peacefully gliding,

The waters dividing,

The indolent bátteau moved slowly along,

The rowers, light-hearted,

From sorrow long parted,

Beguiled the dull moments with laughter and song

"Hurrah for the Rapid! That merrily, merrily

Gambols and leaps on its tortuous way;

Soon we will enter it, cheerily, cheerily,

Pleased with its freshness, and wet with its spray."

More swiftly careering,

The wild Rapid nearing,

They dash down the stream like a terrified steed;

The surges delight them,

No terrors affright them,

Their voices keep pace with the quickening speed:

"Hurrah for the Rapid! That merrily, merrily

Shivers its arrows against us in play;

Now we have entered it, cheerily, cheerily,

Our spirits as light as its feathery spray."

Fast downward they're dashing,

Each fearless eye flashing,

Though danger awaits them on every side;

Yon rock—see it frowning!

They strike—they are drowning!

But downward they speed with the merciless tide:

No voice cheers the Rapid, that angrily, angrily

Shivers their bark in its maddening play;

Gaily they entered it—heedlessly recklessly,

Mingling their lives with its treacherous spray!

湍流颂

一切平静滑过，

水面为之分割，

懒洋洋的小舟慢慢地穿行，

桨手，无忧无虑，

远远离开悲愁，

欢笑歌唱着度过沉闷时刻：

"为湍流欢呼！它快乐地，它快乐地

在曲折路上嬉戏跳跃；

很快我们又将相遇，快活，快活，
为它的鲜活，为它的飞沫。"

灵敏向前滑行，
狂野激流愈近，
湍流像一匹惊马冲刺而下；
汹涌令其愉悦，
它们无所畏惧，
它们高速地行进，发出怒吼：
"为湍流欢呼！它快乐地，它快乐地
调皮地把水剑射向我们；
现在我们终于相遇，快活，快活，
我们轻松如羽毛般的飞沫。"

它们急速地冲下，
眼睛无畏闪烁，
毫不畏惧四面袭来的危险；
岩石——面带不悦！
湍流——它们汹涌！
带着无情的浪潮席卷而下：
无人为湍流喝彩，愤怒地，愤怒地
狂奔着发出它们的怒号；
它们欢欣而来——无心又无情地，
把生命交付四溅的飞沫！

Brock

One voice, one people, —one in heart
    And soul, and feeling, and desire!
    Re-light the smouldering martial fire,
    Sound the mute trumpet, strike the lyre,
    The hero deed cannot expire,
        The dead still play their part.

Raise high the monumental stone!
    A nation's fealty is theirs,
    And we are the rejoicing heirs,
    The honored sons of sires whose cares
    We take upon us unawares,
        As freely as our own.

We boast not of the victory,
    But render homage, deep and just,
    To his—to their—immortal dust,
    Who proved so worthy of their trust
    No lofty pile nor sculptured bust
        Can herald their degree.

No tongue need blazon forth their fame—

The cheers that stir the sacred hill
Are but mere promptings of the will
That conquered then, that conquers still;
And generations yet shall thrill
　　At Brock's remembered name.

Some souls are the Hesperides
　　Heaven sends to guard the golden age,
　　Illuming the historic page
　　With records of their pilgrimage;
　　True Martyr, Hero, Poet, Sage:
　　　　And he was one of these.

Each in his lofty sphere sublime
　　Sit crowned above the common throng,
　　Wrestling with some Pythonic wrong,
　　In prayer, in thunder, thought, or song;
　　Briareus-limbed, they sweep along,
　　　　The Typhons of the time.

奠

一个民族，同声——同心
　　同魂，共情感，同愿望！
　　重燃先辈的斗志之火，

吹响喇叭，拨动竖琴，
　英雄事迹永留存，
　　烈士活在心中。

将纪念碑高高竖起！
　他们为国的忠诚，
　我们欢欣着荣耀着
　继承他们精神的子孙
　我们会将他们事业，
　　自发延续下去。

我们不是吹嘘胜利，
　而是敬意，深沉公正，
　对他——他们——不朽英魂，
　他们值得如此尊敬
　他们的形象远高于
　　雕刻的纪念碑。

无须人为他们宣扬——
　地动山摇的欢呼声
　是他们意志的象征
　昔日无敌，今也无敌；
　世世代代始终缅怀
　　布鲁克的英名。

有些灵魂是上天

　　派来守护家园的神灵，

　　用他们的人生历程

　　点亮人类历史扉页；

　　烈士、英雄、诗人、圣人：

　　　　布鲁克是其一。

每个都代表着崇高，

　　远凌驾于众人之上，

　　敢与错误神谕角力，

　　以祷文、雷电、思想、赞歌；

　　百手巨人，已退场，

　　　　风神时代到来。

　　注：Briareus，希腊神话中的百手巨人；Typhon，希腊神话中的风之父。

The Twofold Victory

By the famous Alma River

　　Knelt a Warrior, brave and young,

Through his veins ran Death's cold shiver,

　　On his lips his last breath hung;

Far above him rolled the battle,

Downward rolled to Alma's wave,
Downward, through the crash and rattle,
    Came the cheering of the brave.

"Comrades," said he, rising slowly,
    Kneeling on one bended knee,
"Comrades," said he, feebly, slowly,
    "Is that cheer for Victory?"
"Yes! —they fly! —the foe is flying!"
    "Comrades," said he, ardently,
"Cheer for me, for I am dying,
    Cheer them on to Victory!"

By that blood-encrimsoned River
    Cheered they with a martial pride,
Death's last shaft had left its quiver,
    And the Warrior, smiling, died.
Faintly his last cheer was given,
    Feebly his last breath went free,
And his spirit passed to Heaven
    On the wings of Victory!

双重的大胜仗

著名的阿尔玛河畔

跪着，年轻的勇士，
死亡在血液里战栗，
　唇边还有一口气；
一直到阿尔玛河畔，
　战斗仍然在继续，
近处，在喧嚣纷杂中，
　传出勇士的欢呼。

"战友们，"他说，缓缓地，
　起身以单膝跪地，
"战友，"他说，脆弱，低声，
　"这是胜利的欢呼？"
"是！——胜了！——敌人逃跑了！"
　"战友，"他说，热情地，
"我快不行了，欢呼吧，
　让我们欢呼胜利！"

在鲜血染红的河边
　军人自豪地欢呼，
死亡最后一次战栗，
　勇士，微笑着，死去。
模糊间听见了欢呼，
　微弱呼吸终停止，
他的灵魂飞上天堂，
　乘着胜利的飞翼！

The Light in the Window Pane

A joy from my soul's departed,
　　A bliss from my heart is flown,
As weary, weary-hearted,
　　I wander alone—alone!
The night wind sadly sigheth
　　A withering, wild refrain,
And my heart within me dieth
　　For the light in the window pane.

The stars overhead are shining,
　　As brightly as e'er they shone,
As heartless, sad, repining,
　　I wander alone—alone!
A sudden flash comes streaming,
　　And flickers adown the lane,
But no more for me is gleaming
　　The light in the window pane.

The voices that pass are cheerful,
　　Men laugh as the night winds moan;
They cannot tell how fearful
　　'Tis to wander alone—alone!

For them, with each night's returning,

　Life singeth its tenderest strain,

Where the beacon of love is burning—

　The light in the window pane.

Oh sorrow beyond all sorrows

　To which human life is prone:

Without thee, through all the morrows,

　To wander alone—alone!

Oh dark, deserted dwelling!

　Where Hope like a lamb was slain,

No voice from thy lone walls welling,

　No light in thy window pane.

But Memory, sainted angel!

　Rolls back the sepulchral stone,

And sings like a sweet evangel:

　"No—never, never alone!

True grief has his royal palace,

　Each loss is a greater gain;

And Sorrow ne'er filled a chalice

　That Joy did not wait to drain!"

窗玻璃透出的光

灵魂的快乐已离去，
　心底的幸福丢失，
心感到疲倦，疲倦，
　我独自漫步——独自！
晚风悲伤叹息
　无力，无控的克制，
而我的心渴望着
　那窗玻璃透出的光。

星星在夜空闪烁，
　光芒明亮如往昔，
胆怯、悲伤和烦闷，
　我独自漫步——独自！
一束光忽然闪过，
　照亮了前面小路，
但是对我而言仍非
　窗玻璃透出的光。

声音传出透着欢喜，
　夜风呜咽人在笑；
不知道多少恐惧
　这独自的漫步——独自！

他们看来，夜会重现，

　　生命之歌最温柔，

爱的灯塔已经被点亮——

　　窗玻璃透出的光。

啊，人的一生总伴随

　　无穷无尽的悲伤：

没有你，剩下的日子，

　　唯独自漫步——独自！

黑暗，无人的公寓！

　　希望消失如灯灭，

屋内没有你的声音，

　　你的窗玻璃无光。

但回忆，如神圣天使！

　　如重石压在心头，

吟唱着甜美的福音：

　　"不！——不要，不要独自！

悲伤应有它的归处，

　　失去意味着获得；

被欢乐耗尽的酒杯

　　终不会填满悲伤。"

The Little Shoes

Her little shoes! We sit and muse
    Upon the dainty feet that wore them;
By day and night our souls' delight
    Is just to dream and ponder o'er them.
We hear them patter on the floor;
    In either hand a toy or rattle;
And what speaks to our hearts the more—
    Her first sweet words of infant prattle.

I see the face so fair, and trace
    The dark-blue eye that flashed so clearly;
The rose-bud lips, the finger-tips
    She learned to kiss—O, far too dearly!
The pearly hands turned up to mine,
    The tiny arms my neck caressing;
Her smile, that made our life divine,
    Her silvery laugh-her kiss, a blessing.

Her winning ways, that made the days
    Elysian in their grace so tender,
Through which Love's child our souls beguiled
    For seeming ages starred with splendor:

No wonder that the angel-heirs

    Did win our darling life's joy from us,

For she was theirs—not all our prayers

    Could keep her from the Land of Promise.

一双小鞋

她的小鞋！我们坐着

    看她穿鞋的秀丽小脚；

日日夜夜我们快乐

    乐于对她双脚的梦与思。

听见它们踏着地板；

    手拿着玩具低声细语；

她甜美的婴儿呢喃——

    完全融化了我们心田。

小脸多么美丽，蓝黑

    双眼清澈如一汪清泉；

玫瑰花唇，娇嫩指尖

    她学着亲吻——噢，好温柔！

嫩白小手牵住我手，

    小小胳膊轻抚我脖颈；

她笑，我们生活绝妙，

    银铃般的声音——吻，是天赐。

她迷人举动，让时光
　　犹如在天堂优雅温柔，
灵魂都因爱而着迷
　　岁月似乎闪耀着光彩：
难怪这小天使收获
　　我们宝贵一生的幸福，
她是天使——我们的祈祷
　　也无法让她离开天堂。

Despondency

There is a sadness o'er my spirit stealing,
　　A flash of fire up-darting to my brain,
Sowing the seeds—and still the seeds concealing—
　　That are to ripen into future pain.
I feel the germs of madness in me springing,
　　Slowly, and certain as the serpent's bound,
And my poor hope, like dying tendrils cling
　　To the green oak, tend surely to the ground;
And Reason's grasps grows feebler day by day,
　　As the slow poison up my nerves is creeping,
Ever and anon through my crushed heart leaping,
　　Like a swift panther darting on its prey;

And the bright taper Hope once fed within,

    Hath waned and perished in the rueful din.

意志消沉

悲伤渐渐偷走了所有的活力，

    像一束火苗投掷进大脑，

投下了颗种子——隐秘的种子——

    终会成长为之后的剧痛。

我感到种子在我体内疯长，

    慢慢地，如一条毒蛇盘踞，

微小的希望，如橡树卷须

    依恋绿树，仍得归于大地；

理智日复一日失去掌控，

    如慢性毒药在血管中蔓延，

又如敏捷的猎豹突袭猎物，

    不久就会击垮我的心脏；

内心曾熊熊的希望之火，

    逐渐熄灭消失于喧嚣中。

The Red-Men—A Sonnet

My footsteps press where, centuries ago,

The Red-Men fought and conquered; lost and won.

Whole tribes and races, gone like last year's snow,

    Have found the Eternal Hunting Grounds, and run

The fiery gauntlet of their active days,

    Till few are left to tell the mournful tale:

And these inspire us with such wild amaze,

    They seem like spectres passing down a vale

Steeped in uncertain moonlight, on their way

    Towards some bourn where darkness blinds the day,

And night is wrapped in mystery profound.

    We cannot lift the mantle of the past:

We seem to wander over hallowed ground:

    We scan the trail of Thought, but all is overcast.

红种人——十四行（诗）

我脚踏之地，在几百年前，

    红种人征服过；胜败寻常。

整个部落，如去年雪不见，

    必是已经觅得了永久，猎场

活跃中经历着火般考验，

    唯幸存者讲述悲伤往事：

这使惊诧情绪疯狂蔓延，

    他们仿佛幽灵走出山地

朦胧月光中，走向目的地

在那里白昼被黑暗遮蔽，
而黑夜包裹在神秘深处。
我们掀不开历史的斗篷：
仿佛漫步在神圣的地域：
搜寻思想的踪迹，却只见迷蒙。

Charles George Douglas Roberts（1860—1943）
查尔斯·乔治·道格拉斯·罗伯茨诗十五首

Afoot

Comes the lure of green things growing,
Comes the call of waters flowing—
And the wayfarer desire
Moves and wakes and would be going.

Hark the migrant hosts of June
Marching nearer noon by noon!
Hark the gossip of the grasses
Bivouacked beneath the moon!

Long the quest and far the ending
When my wayfarer is wending—
When desire is once afoot,
Doom behind and dream attending!

In his ears the phantom chime
Of incommunicable rhyme,
He shall chase the fleeting camp-fires
Of the Bedouins of Time.

Farer by uncharted ways,
Dumb as death to plaint or praise,
Unreturning he shall journey,
Fellow to the nights and days;

Till upon the outer bar
Stilled the moaning currents are,
Till the flame achieves the zenith,
Till the moth attains the star,

Till through laughter and through tears
Fair the final peace appears,
And about the watered pastures
Sink to sleep the nomad years!

徒步

来了那绿色的吸引，
来了流水盈盈呼唤——

徒步者受到吸引
渴望出发开始旅行。

听啊六月的访客
一日一日地走近！
听啊沐浴在月光下
小草在窃窃私语！

当徒步者在旅程中
求索无尽前途漫漫——
在探索的道路上，
厄运远去梦想常伴！

他耳闻的是无法
言语表达出的韵律，
他将追逐贝都因人
时代即逝的营火。

徒步者脚踏荒路，
不顾前途悲或喜，
他义无反顾向前进，
唯日夜星辰为旅；

直至远处的沙洲
咆哮浪潮会平静，

直至火焰熊熊燃烧，
直至飞蛾扑繁星，

直至欢喜与泪水
带来最终的平和，
直到那丰饶的牧场
沉淀了游牧岁月！

An April Adoration

Sang the sun rise on an amber morn—
"Earth, be glad! An April is born."

"Winter's done, and April's in the skies,
Earth, look up with laughter in your eyes!"

Putting off her dumb dismay of snow,
Earth bade all her unseen children grow.

Then the sound of growing in the air
Rose to God a liturgy of prayer;

And the thronged succession of the days
Uttered up to God a psalm of praise.

Laughed the running sap in every vein,
Laughed the running flurries of warm rain,

Laughed the life in every wandering root,
Laughed the tingling cells of bud and shoot.

God all the concord of their mirth
Heard the adoration-song of Earth.

一首四月的赞歌

琥珀色晨曦东升吟起——
　"四月来临。大地，欣喜！"

　"冬日已去，四月正当时，
　眸光欢喜抬眼望，大地！"

摆脱冬雪无声的悲哀，
大地盼着生命的到来。

　万物生长的声音振空
　变成声声祷文传至天庭；

日复一日交织的时光

向着天帝赞美歌高唱。

欢笑的是流动的汁液，
欢笑的是绵绵的春雨，

欢笑的是根脉中的生机，
欢笑的是新萌的嫩枝。

天帝在欢笑中听见
大地对于四月的赞叹。

The Hawkbit

How sweetly on the autumn scene,
When haws are red amid the green,
The hawkbit shines with face of cheer,
The favorite of the faltering year!

When days grow short and nights grow cold,
How fairly gleams its eye of gold
On pastured field and grassy hill,
Along the roadside and the rill!

It seems the spirit of a flower,

This offspring of the autumn hour,
Wandering back to earth to bring
Some kindly afterthought of spring.

A dandelion's ghost might so
Amid Elysian meadows blow,
Become more fragile and more fine
Breathing the atmosphere divine.

蒲公英

秋天景色多么甜美，
山楂为绿枝头缀色，
蒲公英洋溢着欢乐，
是迟暮年中最好的时节！

白天渐短夜晚变凉，
秋天睁开眼眸金亮
凝视着牧场和青山，
照耀了小路和山涧！

它好似一朵花的灵核，
是秋日时节的丰果，
回到大地试图带回
对春天美好的回忆。

蒲公英之魂可能
在绿草的乐土中，
呼吸着神圣的空气
变得更娇嫩更美丽。

The Clearing

Stumps, and harsh rocks, and prostrate trunks all charred
And gnarled roots naked to the sun and rain, —
They seem in their grim stillness to complain,
And be their paint the evening peace is jarred.
These ragged acres fire and the axe have scarred,
And many summers not assuaged their pain.

In vain the pink and saffron light, in vain
The pale dew on the hillocks stripped and marred!
But here and there the waste is touched with cheer
Where spreads the fire-weed like a crimson flood
And venturous plumes of golden-rod appear;
And round the blackened fence the great boughs lean
With comfort; and across the solitude
The hermit's holy transport peals serene.

火烧林

树桩、岩石和匍匐枝烧焦
粗糙树根露于阳光雨水——
它们似沉默不语地抗议，
不平静的傍晚染黑它们。
火和斧头带给土地伤痕，
许多夏日过去疼痛未减。

粉光红光皆无用，山丘上
滴落的苍白露珠也徒劳！
四处可见的荒地欢呼着
火苗像红色的洪水蔓延
金色的柳条如羽毛般飞升；
熏黑的篱笆旁倒着树枝
平静躯干；孤独的另一边
蜂鸟神圣翅膀灼伤宁静。

Grey Rocks, and Greyer Sea

Grey rocks, and greyer sea,
And surf along the shore—
And in my heart a name

My lips shall speak no more.

The high and lonely hills

Endure the darkening year—

And in my heart endure

A memory and a tear.

Across the tide a sail

That tosses, and is gone—

And in my heart the kiss

That longing dreams upon.

Grey rocks, and greyer sea,

And surf along the shore—

And in my heart the face

That I shall see no more.

灰色岩，灰色海

灰色岩，灰色海,
沿着海岸冲击——
心中有个名字
双唇无法吐露。
那些孤寂高山
忍受黑暗之年——
在我心里藏着
一段回忆伴着泪。
横渡海浪的帆

被倾覆，已死去——
我的心里藏着
被亲吻的渴望。
灰色岩，灰色海，
沿着海岸冲击——
我心里那张脸
我再也见不到。

At the Gates of Spring

With April here,

And first thin green on the awakening bough,

What wonderful things and dear,

My tired heart to cheer,

At last appear,

Colours of dream afloat on cloud and tree,

So far, so clear,

A spell, a mystery;

And joys that thrill and sing,

New come on mating wing,

The wistfulness and ardour of the spring—

And Thou!

春天的入口

四月来临，
唤醒春枝点缀上一分薄绿，
多么绝妙又宝贵，
去心之倦意，
春意终至，
彩色的梦飘浮云端树梢，
遥远，清晰，
迷人，而且神秘；
歌声透着喜意，
落在交叠鸟翼，
春天带来了渴望与激情——
和你！

Hilltop Song

When the lights come out in the cottages
Along the shores at eve,
And across the darkening water
The last pale colours leave;

And up from the rock-ridged pasture slopes
The sheep-bell tinklings steal,
And the folds are shut, and the shepherds
Turn to their quiet meal;

And even here, on the unfenced height,
No journeying wind goes by,
But the earth-sweet smells and the home-sweet sounds
Mount, like prayer, to the sky;

Then from the door of my opened heart
Old blindness and pride are driven,
Till I know how high is the humble,
The dear earth how close to heaven.

山巅颂

傍晚海岸上的小木屋里
投射出了灯光，
暗沉的海面最后一色
苍白终于消去；

绿草茵茵的山坡高处
羊铃声已不再，
羊圈紧闭，牧人静静地

围坐吃着晚餐；

这里，没有篱笆的高处，
晚风虽没有拂过，
泥土的清香和生活气息
如祷文，飞升入天；

只有盲目与骄傲离开
我那敞开着的心门，
我才知道谦逊的高贵，
大地天堂咫尺相邻。

Monition

A faint wind, blowing from World's End,
Made strange the city street.
A strange sound mingled in the fall
Of the familiar feet.
Something unseen whirled with the leaves
To tap on door and sill.
Something unknown went whispering by
Even when the wind was still.
And men looked up with startled eyes
And hurried on their way,

As if they had been called, and told
How brief their day.

天之谕

微风，来自世界尽头，
街道变得陌生。
熟悉的脚步声中
夹杂陌生之音。
不知道何物与树叶
飞旋轻击窗门。
风虽静仍旧传来莫名
事物的低语声。
路上行人步履匆匆
惊异抬眼望去，
似乎被召唤，被告知
光阴飞逝。

The Frosted Pane

One night came Winter noiselessly, and leaned
Against my window-pane.
In the deep stillness of his heart convened
The ghosts of all his slain.

Leaves, and ephemera, and stars of earth,

And fugitives of grass, —

White spirits loosed from bonds of mortal birth,

He drew them on the glass.

窗上霜华

冬天悄悄到来在一夜间，

倚靠我的窗棂。

他在宁静心灵深处召唤

他带走的魂灵。

树叶、浮游生物、点点繁星、

草丛中的生灵——

脱离生死束缚白色精灵，

被他画在窗棂。

The Herring Weir

Back to the green deeps of the outer bay

The red and amber currents glide and cringe,

Diminishing behind a luminous fringe

Of cream-white surf and wandering wraiths of spray.

Stealthily, in the old reluctant way,

The red flats are uncovered, mile on mile,

To glitter in the sun a golden while.
Far down the flats, a phantom sharply grey,
The herring weir emerges, quick with spoil.
Slowly the tide forsakes it. Then draws near,
Descending from the farm-house on the height,
A cart, with gaping tubs. The oxen toil
Sombrely o'er the level to the weir,
And drag a long black trail across the light.

在鲱鱼堰

回望海湾外的绿色深处，
红琥珀色潮水时进时退，
渐渐消失在连成一线不住
徘徊的奶白色的浪花背面。
慢慢地如过去般，不得不，
露出红色平地，数英里远，
阳光下闪耀着金色光芒。
平地的深处，是一个灰影，
鲱鱼堰出现，很快又隐去。
慢慢被潮水抛弃。牛拉车
从高处的农舍缓缓向下
驶来，车斗破裂。牛慢悠悠
经过水边慢慢走向鲱鱼堰，
拖着长长黑影穿过晚霞。

Twilight on Sixth Avenue at Ninth Street

Over the tops of the house
　Twilight and sunset meet.
The green, diaphanous dusk
　Sinks to the eager street.

Astray in the tangle of roofs
　Wanders a wind of June.
The dial shines in the clock-tower
　Like the face of a strange-scrawled moon.

The narrowing lines of the houses
　Palely begin to gleam,
And the hurrying crowds fade softly
　Like an army in a dream.

Above the vanishing faces
　A phantom train flares on
With a voice that shakes the shadows, —
　Diminishes, and is gone.

And I walk with the journeying throng
　In such a solitude

As where a lonely ocean
　　Washes a lonely wood.

九号街第六大道的暮色

排排屋顶的上空
　　暮光落日相交。
绿，朦胧的暮色
　　沉入热闹街道。

六月风游荡迷失
　　在交织的街畔。
钟塔的钟面发着光
　　像潦草画出的月盘。

房屋似乎被细线勾勒
　　渐露苍白光影，
匆匆的人群如梦中
　　的军队失去踪影。

消失的脸庞上方
　　幽灵火车忽至
声响之大惊动阴影——
　　它逐渐隐去，消逝。

走在过往的人群中
　我却如此孤独
就像孤独的海水
　流过一棵独木。

In an Old Barn

Tons upon tons the brown-green fragrant hay,
O'erbrims the mows beyond the time-warped eaves,
Up to the rafters where the spider weaves,
Though few flies wander his secluded way.
Through a high chink one lonely golden ray,
Wherein the dust is dancing, slants unstirred.
In the dry hush some rustlings light are heard,
Of winter-hidden mice at furtive play.
Far down, the cattle in their shadowed stalls,
Nose-deep in clover fodder's meadowy scent,
Forget the snows that whelm their pasture streams,
The frost that bites the world beyond their walls.
Warm housed, they dream of summer, well content
In day-long contemplation of their dreams.

在旧谷仓

成吨的棕绿芬芳的干草，
高过被时间扭曲的屋檐，
直碰到蜘蛛织网的橡木，
苍蝇不会飞到的孤独处。
一束金光透过高处缝隙，
尘土飞扬，斜射光线不动。
寂静中传来窸窣的响声，
畏寒的老鼠在偷偷玩耍。
远处，牛在阴暗畜栏里，
鼻子深埋在清香草料中，
忘了覆盖牧场溪流的雪，
和墙外世界肆虐的霜冻。
居暖室，梦夏日，如此满足
它们整日沉迷于美梦中。

The Aim

O thou who lovest not alone
The swift success, the instant goal,
But hast a lenient eye to mark
The failures of th' inconstant soul,

Consider not my little worth, —

The mean achievement, scamped in act

The high resolve and low result,

The dream that durst not face the fact.

But count the reach of my desire.

Let this be something in Thy sight: —

I have not, in the slothful dark,

Forgot the Vision and the Height.

Neither my body nor my soul

To earth's low ease will yield consent.

I praise Thee for my will to strive.

I bless Thy goad of discontent.

目标

哦，并非就你渴望

瞬间命中，成功迅速，

但也要宽容地看待

你无常的灵魂失误，

我这个人微不足道——

拙劣行动，平庸成就

高目标结局却失意，
梦想总与现实脱钩。

想想我的所求所图。
让它进入你的眼帘——
慵懒的黑暗中，我未
忘记了高度和远见。

无论身体还是灵魂
都不会屈服于安逸。
赞美你赋予的斗志。
祝福你带来的激励。

The Potato Harvest

A high bare field, brown from the plough, and borne

Aslant from sunset; amber wastes of sky

Washing the ridge; a clamour of crows that fly

In from the wide flats where the spent tides mourn

To yon their rocking roosts in pines wind-torn;

A line of grey snake-fence, that zigzags by

A pond and cattle; from the homestead nigh

The long deep summonings of the supper horn.

Black on the ridge, against that lonely flush,

A cart, and stoop-necked oxen; ranged beside
Some barrels; and the day-worn harvest-folk,
Here emptying their baskets, jar the hush
With hollow thunders. Down the dusk hillside
Lumbers the wain; and day fades out like smoke.

马铃薯大丰收

光秃高地，褐土，日影西斜
琥珀色残阳；笼罩着山脊
鸦群；自广阔的平原上飞来，
以喧闹的鸦啼声音哀悼
被风摧残摇摇欲坠窝巢；
还有灰色的篱笆、池塘及
牛群蜿蜒，远远传来农户
那回家吃晚餐的呼唤声。
幽暗山脊，伴着寂寞晚霞，
马车，吃草的牛群；一排排
木桶；劳累了一天的人们，
清空篮筐，在寂静里填满
轰轰雷鸣。星辰缓缓爬上
山坡；日光如烟火般消散。

The Great and Little Weavers

The great and the little weavers,
They neither rest nor sleep.
They work in the height and the glory,
They toil in the dark and the deep.
The rainbow melts with the shower,
The white-thorn falls in the gust,
The cloud-rose dies into shadow,
The earth-rose dies into dust.
But they have not faded forever,
They have not flowered in vain,
For the great and the little weavers
Are weaving under the rain.

Recede the drums of the thunder
When the titan chorus tires,
And the bird-song piercing the sunset
Faints with the sunset fires,

But the trump of the storm shall fail not,
Nor the flute-cry fails of the thrush,
For the great and the little weavers
Are weaving under the hush.

The comet flares into darkness,
The flame dissolves into death,
The power of the star and the dew
They glow and are gone like a breath,

But ere the old wonder is done
Is the new-old wonder begun,
For the great and the little weavers
Are weaving under the sun.

The domes of an empire crumble,
A child's hope dies in tears;
Time rolls them away forgotten
In the silt of the flooding years;

The creed for which men died smiling
Decays to a beldame's curse;
The love that made lips immortal
Drags by in a tattered hearse.

But not till the search of the moon
Sees the last white face uplift,
And over the bones of the kindreds
The bare sands dredge and drift,

Shall love forget to return

And lift the unused latch,

(In his eyes the look of the traveller,

On his lips the foreign catch),

Nor the mad song leaves men cold,

Nor the high dream summon in vain, —

For the great and the little weavers

Are weaving in heart and brain.

伟大渺小的织工

伟大而渺小的织工，

他们不眠不休，

他们工作在高光中，

他们劳作在幽暗处。

阵雨融化了彩虹，

狂风吹落了棘刺，

天上云消逝于阴影，

地上花零落成泥。

但它们不会就此褪色，

它们不无意开花，

因为伟大渺小的织工

在雨中忙着编织。

太阳的合奏声疲惫
雷声此时也消退，
忽闻鸟鸣声穿透夕阳
带走落日余晖。

暴风雨不会就此停歇，
画眉鸟儿歌唱不止，
因为伟大渺小的织工
仍在静静地编织。

彗星光亮坠入黑暗，
火焰渐暗至死亡，
星星与露珠闪耀着的
光芒如呼吸般消亡。

旧的精彩之作未完
新的作品已经开始，
因为伟大渺小的织工
在太阳光下编织。

帝国的穹顶已坍塌，
孩童希望破灭；
时光带走所有一切
葬于洪流下的淤泥；

愿以命为持的信条
堕落成恶毒诅咒；
令双唇不朽的爱情
被破旧灵车拖走。

月光下见到最后那
白皙的脸庞抬起，
在祖祖辈辈的尸骨上
只有沙土飘移，

爱是否忘记回转
拉开久闭门闩，
（他一眼看到的是名游子，
口中是外来之物）
放声歌唱人心暖，
崇高理想鼓舞士气——
因为伟大渺小的织工
在尽心尽力编织。

John McCrae（1872—1918）
约翰·麦克雷诗一首

Disarmament

One spake amid the nations, "Let us cease
　　From darkening with strife the fair
　　　　World's light,
We who are great in war be great in peace.
　　No longer let us plead the cause by might."

But from a million British graves took birth
　　A silent voice—the million spake as one—
"If ye have righted all the wrongs of earth
　　Lay by the sword! Its work and ours is done."

放下武器

有人在国际上呼吁："停火

武装冲突已使光明
　　暗淡，
战时强者将兴盛于和平。
　　不要再以武力作为托言。"

英国百万将士坟墓发出
　　无声的号召——众口如一声——
　　"如果你已纠正战争错误
　　　躺在剑旁！我们使命完成。"

Norman Bethune（1890—1939）
诺尔曼·白求恩诗六首

Red Moon

And this same pallid moon tonight,
  Which rides so quietly, clear and high,
The mirror of our pale and troubled gaze,
  Raised to the cool Canadian sky,

Above the shattered Spanish mountain tops
  Last night, rose low and wild and red,
Reflecting back from her illumined shield,
  The blood bespattered faces of the dead.

To that pale disc, we raised our clenched fists
  And to those nameless dead our vows renew,
"Comrades, who fought for freedom and the future world,
  Who died for us, we will remember you."

红月

今夜同样苍凉的月，
　如此寂静，皎洁高悬，
映着暗淡忧虑的眼神，
　挂在加国清冷天边。

昨夜月亮低垂西班牙
　破碎高山之巅，血红。
她光洁的盾牌上反射出，
　逝者鲜血溅污的面容。

向苍白月盘，举起怒拳
　我们向无名的死者宣誓：
"同志们，他们为自由未来而战，
　为我们牺牲，我们将牢记。"

A Poem to Pony

My pony is a bird in my hand
Fluttering,
Beating her wings,
Not to be held.

My Pony is a tree in the wind,
Dancing,
Bowing and swaying
Not to be broken.

My Pony is a wave in the sea
Sweeping
Across the deep wastes
Not to be hindered.

My pony is a gleam in the dark,
Shining,
A dart, a flash of sun
Then done.

My Pony is not for love,
Invulnerable,
Yet her I love
or no one.

致波妮的诗句

我的波妮像我掌中鸟
振翅飞，
扇动翅膀，
不喜束缚。

我的波妮是狂风中的
大树，
弯曲又摇摆
不愿被折服。

我的波妮是海中浪潮
激荡，
突破那沙漠
她无可阻挡。

我的波妮是黑暗里的
亮光，
是箭，一束阳光
闪过。

波妮不为爱而生，
她如此坚强，
无人如我
深爱她。

Untitled

My pony is a bird,

You find it strange that
Hooves should beat, like wings,
The sky?

My pony is a flower
'Tis odd, is't not,
Her eyes should shine
Like stars?

My pony is a cloud
How strange her feet should be
So firmly fixed in
The deep earth?

My pony is all of these—
And none—so strange a flame.
Myself—my own—unknown
My sister and my bride.

无题诗

我的波妮是鸟，
是否很奇怪
脚，能像翅膀，
振空？

我的波妮是鲜花
奇怪，是吗，
双眸闪耀
星光？

我的波妮是云
为何她的双脚
能稳稳踏入
厚土中？

我的波妮是一切——
又非——神奇火焰。
而我——不知——她是
姐妹还是新娘。

Remembrance

I can't pretend
I think of you every hour.
Why some dull days I'm not aware of you at all,
Any more than the beating of my heart.
Then, a young tree in the wind,
A white flower in the grass,

A quick bird in flight,

A breath of sun-warmed air,

And the whole world is emptied of delight

Like a cup turned upside down

And I am hollowed and sick for my love.

But I can't pretend

This happens every day,

My pony.

想念你

不能佯装
我时刻在想念你。
为何暗淡的日子里未惦念你，
竟然多于我自己的心跳。
然而，风中的小树，
草丛中的小白花，
疾飞的小鸟，
日光下的空气，
整个世界像倒置的水杯
失去所有的愉悦
即使我因爱而心绪不宁。
却不能佯装
我每日都如此，
想波妮。

To Pony

Hand clasped
Look, see us stand, with eager upturned faces
Lit by the rising sun of our new love,
Whose gentle light touches so tenderly
Eyelids and mouth.

O, my sweet, I am afraid
That soon, perhaps, his mounting rays
Now roseate and kind
Will, in the high noon of passionate desire,
Strike down, with shafts of molten fire
Our bared, defenceless heads,
And neath those blazing beams, we languish and despair
Too eager then his course should run
Into the west and harm us once again
In the cool shade of well-remembered trees,
Alone and separate.

Dare we hold high our unprotected heads
Or, warmed by the memory of other dawns
Behind us, smile gently, part and go our ways,
Across the waste land of the years

Carefree and undisturbed.

Or stay instead and unafrighted, cry
Come light of love and life, shine down,
STRIKE, if strike you must
But warm us first, 'twas better so to die
Beneath your fierce flames than perish in the shade,
Cold and alone.

Perhaps a miracle as happened once, should come again
That golden globe were made to stand
And never sink and never leave the land
Desolate and dark. But stay, suspended overhead,
High, serene and clear perpetuate.

致波妮

牵手
看，我们站着，仰着热情的脸
焕发着爱情萌芽的红光，
这光如此温柔地触摸
眼睑和唇。

啊，亲爱的，我担忧
可能，此刻，愈加强烈

美好的光线
将会，在激情的正午中消退，
炽热的火焰击打着
大脑，毫无防备，
在如此强光中，备受煎熬绝望
感情太热烈而最终
消退而带来一次次伤害
在那记忆深处的树荫下，
苦尝孤独寂寥。

我们是否敢高昂着头颅
或，因为以往记忆中的温暖
面带温柔的笑意，各自前行，
无忧无虑泰然自若
穿过岁月荒原。

要么就勇敢地留下，呼唤
爱与生命之光，照耀，
击退，击退前
请赐温暖，宁愿在烈焰中
死去也不愿在寒冷孤寂中，
黯然而去。

也许曾经的奇迹，还将会再次发生
让金色火球永不熄

绝不离开这片荒凉
大地。那么留下来吧，在空中高悬，
皎洁而宁静，永垂不朽。

I Come from Cuatro Caminos

I come from Cuatro Caminos,
From Cuatro Caminos I come,
My eyes are overflowing,
And clouded with blood.
The blood of a little fair one,
Whom I saw destroyed on the ground;
The blood of a young woman,
The blood of an old man, a very old man,
The blood of many people, of many
Trusting, helpless,
Fallen under the bombs
Of the pirates of the air.
I come from Cuatro Caminos,
From Cuatro Caminos I come,
My ears are deaf
With blasphemies and wailings
Ay Little One, Little One;
What hast thou done to these dogs

That they have dashed thee in pieces

On the stones of the ground?

Ay, ay, ay. Mother, my Mother!

Why have they killed the old grandfather?

Because they are wolf's cubs,

Cubs of a man-eating wolf.

Because the blood that runs in their veins

Is blood of brothel and mud

Because in their regiment they were born fatherless

A "curse on God" rends the air

Towards the infamy of Heaven.

啊，库亚特罗·卡米诺斯

啊，库亚特罗·卡米诺斯，

这是我所居住的地方，

我的眼睛在流血，

模糊了双眼。

是可爱的孩童的血，

他被炸死，躺在地上；

是年轻女人的血，

是个很老、很老的人的鲜血，

是无数无助，急需帮助的

人们的血，

他们倒在那些

掠夺者的炸弹下。

啊，库亚特罗·卡米诺斯，

这是我所居住的地方，

到处哭号

震耳欲聋的罪恶

唉，孩子啊，孩子啊；

你到底错在哪里

以至于那些狗将你

扑倒在石地上？

唉，唉，唉。妈妈，妈妈呀！

它们为何杀死老祖父？

因是狼的幼崽，

吃人的狼的后代。

因为它们血管里流动

的是罪恶与污秽

因为在它们狼群

天生无父教养

对天帝发出咒骂

撕裂天空亵渎了天庭。

Dorothy Livesay（1909—1996）
多萝西·利夫赛诗一首

Green Rain

I remember long veils of green rain
Feathered like the shawl of my grandmother—
Green from the half-green of the spring trees
Waving in the valley.

I remember the road
Like the one which leads to my grandmother's house,
A warm house, with green carpets,
Geraniums, a trilling canary
And shining horse-hair chairs;
And the silence, full of the rain's falling
Was like my grandmother's parlour
Alive with herself and her voice, rising and falling—
Rain and wind intermingled.

I remember on that day

I was thinking only of my love

And of my love's house.

But now I remember the day

As I remember my grandmother.

I remember the rain as the feathery fringe of her shawl.

绿雨

我记得绿雨的长围巾

毛茸茸犹如祖母的披巾——

绿油油如春树的半绿

在山谷中摇摆。

我记得那条路

如通往祖母房子的那条路，

暖暖的，铺着地毯，

天竺葵，低鸣的金丝雀

闪光的马鬃沙发；

一片宁静，充满沥沥雨声

犹如祖母的大客厅

充满她的身影和声音，时高时低——

雨和风交织在一起。

我记得在那天
心中只想着我的恋人
和他的房子。
现在我想起那一天
就好像想起我的祖母。
我记得雨如她披巾上羽毛似的饰边。

译后记

翻译英语诗歌，并非一时兴起。译诗作诗，大概是每个文艺青年的梦想。1972年，我还在四川宜宾的一所中学读高中。当时，国家重新开始大学招生（"文革"中的第一批工农兵学员自这一年开始），并考虑让高中毕业生参加高考。这个好消息给了我那一代的青年学子莫大的希望。宜宾地区的教育部门还专门为我们这些1971年4月入学的"文革"开始后的第一批二年制的高中班级增加了半年的学习时间，期望我们可以参加可能于1973年举行的高考。但是，在1973年的考试中，"白卷英雄"横空出世，彻底打破了我们这些求知若渴的在读高中生通过考试上大学的梦想。1973年7月，我高中毕业了。由于宜宾地区比四川省其他地区提前一年招收高中生，我必须等待全省的统一安排——无论是就业还是上山下乡，都要等到一年后省内其他地区的高中生毕业后统一进行。我立刻面临着毕业即无业的境地。没有书读，没有工作，连上山下乡都要等至少一年以后。作为同年级中"又红又专"的学生（除了体育，在校期间的每次考试，我的各门功课成绩都是年级第一，而且几乎门门满分；在校期间，我还曾当过宜宾市团代会代表），因此我所受打击之大难以言表。我之后就是在工厂里做临时工，什么体力活都干过，从最初挑 40 公斤东西，到后来挑 130 公斤河沙。4 个人抬条石，重达 500 公斤，我可以轻易抬起；200 多公斤的碱水桶，我和同伴两个人就能抬起，而且走的都是从河边到工厂区的上坡路。19 岁年轻人的肩膀挑起了生活的重担。繁重的劳动，单调的生活，心中的苦恼，自然激发起了对诗的梦想。想到前途茫茫无望，想到从首都北京流落到四川偏僻的小城，从小学三年级就开始学的法语因为没有语言环境已经忘得差不多了（我 1964 年 9 岁时进的北京外国语学院附属外国语学校），落差之大让我不由得诗兴大发。还记得，当时心情郁闷的我曾经写过一首诗，题名《路的选择》，和弗罗斯特的"The Road Not Taken"（《未选择之路》）何其相似。可惜的是，因为多次搬家，原稿早已不知去向。

1976 年，我终于迎来了拨乱反正的历史时刻。1977 年，高考恢复。我有幸成为"文革"后第一届进入大学的 77 级学生，来到了西南地区知名学府四川大学，进入外文系英文专业学习，终于成为一个名副其实的大学生。在 4 年的大学学习中，我初心未改，依然热衷于文学——从最初的一般涉猎，到后来直接啃大部头原著，广泛阅读了当时图书馆所能借到的英美文学名著。在读到弗罗斯特的"The Road Not Taken"时，我真是感慨万分，深感文学是无国界的，人类的情感是相通的，随之产生了翻译介绍英美诗歌的想法。然而，1982 年 1 月毕业后，我被分配到一所工科大学（当时名叫重庆交通学院），从事大学英语教学工作，我的文学梦就戛然而止。

翻译工作是做过的，但那是科技翻译——我曾为钱伟长任主编的《应用数学和力学》（月刊，中英文版在国内外同时出版发行）审读论文长达八年，合计审读了大约2000万字。11年后的1993年，我调到了浙江大学，曾打算重拾文学研究和文学翻译之梦，但是出于工作原因，我的文学梦依然遥遥无期。退休以后，我总算有了闲暇，可以做点自己想做的事。文学之梦再次燃起。当然，作诗写小说的激情早已不再。不过，几十年的英语教学与研究，以及后来同时从事的汉语国际教育的教学与研究，为我从事翻译奠定了坚实的基础。我遂开始翻译一些英美诗人的短诗。2019年，北京外国语大学（原名北京外国语学院）附属外国语学校举行建校六十周年校庆，组委会打算出一本诗文集以纪念我们这所特殊的学校（该校曾因故于1988年停办）。此前在2005年和2014年的校庆活动中，组委会出版了《天上的学校》（中国电影出版社，2006）和《吾时念》（内部发行）两本纪念文集，我曾提供了几篇文章。这次，文集的组织者、文学才子、我的同班同学刘惠杰再次希望我为文集做点儿贡献。我不得不告知，创作的东西，没有，仅有的文学成果就是正在翻译的几位英美诗人的诗作，不知是否可以接受。他慨然应允。我遂将已经完成翻译的弗罗斯特的几首诗（当然也包括我特别钟爱的那首"The Road Not Taken"的译文）发给了他。不久后他又"得寸进尺"，希望我用英语翻译该文集的开篇，作为"课堂作业"的诗歌——苏轼的《赤壁怀古》。朋友之情不能辜负，我勉强交上了一篇凑数。之后，我又陆续翻译了一百多首狄金森的短诗。我本打算出一本英美短诗选译，了结大学时代的诗歌翻译梦后即收手，但在和出版社编辑讨论时发现，采用双语版方式，弗罗斯特和狄金森的短诗已经差不多可以凑成一本了。因此，我干脆补译了几十首美国诗歌，合成一册出版。而英国诗歌则继续翻译，另出一册。因此也就有了两本英美短诗选译：《美诗佳韵》和《英诗佳韵》。

黄杲炘先生在其专著《英诗汉译学》（上海外语教育出版社，2007；2020 修订本）中，系统介绍了英诗汉译的五种方法："民族化译法""自由化译法""字数相应译法""以顿代步译法""兼顾顿数与字数译法"。这五种译法，各有特点，译者们也有各自的选择。本人在几经斟酌之后，决定采用"字数相应译法"中的最初模式，即"字数相等译法"，也就是一个英语音节用一个汉字译出，完全按照"1:1"的方式翻译英语诗歌，这样可以达到一音对一音的效果，让读者在一定程度上感受到英语诗歌节奏之美。前辈诗歌翻译大师如朱湘、戴镏龄、施颖洲、高健等都曾用这一方法翻译过一些英美诗歌。在译诗时，我对所选英美诗歌均采用"字数相等译法"翻译，并将这一方法发挥到了极致，包括每首诗的标题也同样采用此译法。

采用"字数相等译法"可以在视觉上还原英语诗歌的形式美。但是，英诗在格律上和汉语诗歌各有特点。汉语以字为单位，汉诗每行的字数从上古的二言体、三言体发展到《诗经》的四言体，之后发展到唐代的以五言体和七言体（二字音组或三字音组）为主。而词曲则继承了《楚辞》的口语化节奏体系，不限顿的字数（顿的音节容量增多加大），不限诗行的音节数。（许霆：《中国新诗的韵律节奏论》，北京师范大学出版社，2016）英语以音节为单位，构成英诗的节奏的基础是韵律（metre），各行讲究一定的音节数量。英语的诗句，按音节和重音计算韵律，度量韵律的单位为音步（foot）。每个音步由一个重读音节和一个或多个非重读音节构成。重读音节为扬，非重读音节为抑，在英诗中按规律交替出现。英诗中的音步常用的有抑扬格、扬抑格、扬抑抑格、抑扬抑格等，由此产生英诗的节奏美。诗行的长短以音步数目计算，有单音步诗、二音步诗、三音步诗、四音步诗，甚至八音步诗等。（罗良功：《英诗概论》，武汉大学出版社，2002）这样，每行的音节数可以是二到十甚至二十多不等。

由于汉诗和英诗的节奏韵律并不相同，因此，完全按照"1∶1"的方式翻译英语诗歌，也只能在一定程度上体现英语诗歌的节奏韵律。这种译法，也无法顾及英诗的音步，难以体现英诗的轻重音以表现其抑扬顿挫之感。另外，英诗往往用词精练，单音节词居多，尤其早期英诗更是如此，甚至有的英诗每行都是单音节词，这样的诗句往往很难完全按照"1∶1"的方式翻译。尽管如此，我还是坚持完全按照"1∶1"的方式翻译英诗，以求在一定程度上为读者还原英诗的节奏韵律之美。当然，对诗歌的选择因此受到了一些限制。

押韵和节奏一样，是诗歌的基本特征之一，可以表现诗歌的音乐性。押韵可以使诗歌容易朗读和背诵，使诗歌流畅，富有韵味。（聂珍钊：《英语诗歌形式导论》，中国社会科学出版社，2007）由于汉英语音系统的不同，英诗的一些音韵形式在汉语中很难表现出来，如英诗中行中韵里的头韵（alliteration）、元韵（assonance）、辅韵（consonance）等。英诗和汉诗类似的是尾韵(end rhyme),但其格式也不尽相同。此外,英诗中还有很多无韵诗。对于音韵,我在翻译中尽量保持原来的尾韵;对于无韵诗,则按照汉语诗歌押韵的一般方式,尽量在双数行押韵,从而使译文保持一定的音乐性。

诗歌作为一种特殊的文学形式,其意义很难从构筑诗歌的文字符号字面上去理解。诗歌的意义可以分为三个层次:字面意义、感官意义和情感意义。中国有"诗言志""诗者,吟咏性情也"等说法,英语诗歌当然也不例外。英国诗人济慈说,"诗的生命在于热情";另一位英国诗人柯尔律治则指出,"诗歌是再现自然环境和人类思想感情的艺术"。诗歌意义的表现形式主要有:模糊、反语、似是而非。(罗良功:《英诗概论》,武汉大学出版社,2002)美国诗人弗罗斯特则认为:"隐喻,即指东说西,以此述彼,隐喻的欢欣。诗简直就是由隐喻构成的……每首诗在其本质上都是一个新的隐喻,不然就什么都不是。"(弗罗斯特:《弗罗斯特集:诗全集、散文和戏剧作品》,曹明伦译,辽宁教育出版社,2002)因此,在翻译中要准确地表达原作者的本意是很难的。也正因为如此,才有弗罗斯特的名言:诗歌是翻译后失去的东西。尽管诗歌翻译很难,但是,为了不同国家和民族的人们欣赏和体味其他国家和民族的优秀诗歌作品,历代译者仍然不遗余力地在诗歌翻译领域艰难跋涉。我在翻译这些诗歌的时候,也在尽力还原作者的本意。希望这一努力能够得到读者的认同。

在出版了《美诗佳韵》和《英诗佳韵》后,我感到还应该翻译其他几个英语国家的诗歌。因此我和我曾经的学生,现在浙江科技大学外国语学院任教的连巧红一起选译了澳大利亚、新西兰和加拿大三国的一百多首英语诗歌，从而有了这本《澳新加诗佳韵》。这样，世界上五个主要英语国家的诗歌，我们都有所涉猎。其中，最令我们欣喜的是，我们翻译了在中国家喻户晓的加拿大共产党党员、国际主义战士诺尔曼·白求恩大夫的全部六首诗歌，让读者可以一睹这位国际知名的外科医生、坚定的共产主义者不为人知的充满人情和激情的另一面。本书中的诗歌主要由连巧红翻译，我也参与了其中一些诗歌的翻译，并对全书的译文进行了审校。澳大利亚、新西兰和加拿大三个国家的英语诗歌翻译与英国和美国的诗歌翻译相比，在国内虽不是空白，但是确实鲜见，尤其是新西兰诗歌的翻译，更是少之又少。这些都给我们的资料查找和翻译工作带来了很大的不便。我们希望拙译能起到抛砖引玉之功，为我国的英语诗歌翻译略尽绵薄之力，也期盼有更多的翻译学者涉足这三个国家的诗歌翻译和研究。

最后，我要向诸葛勤先生表示诚挚的感谢。我们是多年的朋友和同事（他曾在浙江大学外国语学院工作多年），二十多年来，他参与了我几十本教材、教学参考书和专著的策划及编辑工作。在临近退休之际，他还不辞辛劳地担任了本书的责任编辑。这几本书的书名也出自他的提议。他的真知灼见，以及辛勤而细致的工作为本书增添了魅力。

黄建滨

2024 年于杭州西湖区求是村